Palm Beach
Entertains

THEN AND NOW

Palm Beach
Entertains

THEN AND NOW

*The Junior League
of the Palm Beaches, Inc.*

Coward, McCann & Geoghegan, Inc.
New York

Library of Congress Cataloging in Publication Data

Junior League of the Palm Beaches.
  Palm Beach entertains.

  Includes index.
  1. Cookery, American—Florida. 2. Palm Beach, Fla.—
History. I. Title.
TX715.J9745   1976   641.5   76-16002
SBN: 698-10748-9

PRINTED IN THE UNITED STATES OF AMERICA

THE JUNIOR LEAGUE OF THE PALM BEACHES, INC.

Chairman: Mrs. George G. Matthews
Editor, writer: Mrs. John T. Murray
Recipe coordinator: Mrs. Gary Wiren
Copy editor: Mrs. Harrison K. Chauncey, Jr.

Research and interviewing: Mrs. David Reese, Mrs. Dan H. Campbell

Testing chairmen: Mrs. J. Roy Duke, Mrs. Charles M. Huttig, Jr.,
Mrs. Peter A. Manz, Mrs. Michael Peters, Mrs. Raymond F. Blosser,
Mrs. Edward W. Crawford, Mrs. Harry W. Massey,
Mrs. Wyckoff Myers, Mrs. B. F. Paty, Jr., Mrs. G. David Raymond,
Mrs. Moritz Schultz, and Mrs. A. Ward Wagner, Jr.

Committee: Mrs. E. Llwyd Ecclestone, Jr., Miss Danielle Harris,
Mrs. Lawrence C. Freer and Ms. Sally Shuster.

Food consultant: Maurice Moore-Betty

The Junior League of the Palm Beaches is an educational and charitable organization whose purpose is to promote voluntarism, to develop the potential of its members for voluntary participation in community affairs, and to demonstrate the effectiveness of trained volunteers. The proceeds from the book will be used to finance the League's projects within the community.

Contents

PART 1

Palm Beach
Entertained

Many things have changed since shortly before the beginning of this century when the first group of discriminating pleasure seekers came to South Florida following the warm rays of the sun. However, one thing that has remained constant is the magic and myth embodied in the name Palm Beach, a name that has cast a spell since the area first attracted people seeking a haven of repose and respite from their cares and obligations.

The lure of Palm Beach has lasted for almost a century, and in an era of changing tastes, the name Palm Beach has remained synonymous with luxury and style. Its renown is rooted in its heritage: a wildly beautiful semitropical island transformed from its primitive state to America's most exclusive winter resort, a hotel community that under the architectural guidance of Addison Mizner would become a medieval city and the bastion of the socially prominent. Today, Palm Beach means glamor and sophistication—it is a reputation based on the discriminating tastes of contemporary Palm Beachers, but is well fortified with the remembrances of the town's opulent past, for Palm Beach today is a unique combination of the present and the past.

During the first half of the nineteenth century the tropical wilderness of South Florida lay asleep in the sun virtually undisturbed. Civilization had come to Northern Florida hand in hand with the growth and development of the bordering states, but the Southern portion of the peninsula remained untouched by white men until the Seminole uprisings of the 1830s, when army troops were sent into the marshy grasslands to subdue the rebellious Indians. Colonel William Jenkins Worth brought the Seminole war to a successful conclusion in 1842, and the large freshwater lake lying between the mainland and a coastal chain of limestone and coral islands, extending twenty-two miles from the present towns of Juno Beach to Boynton Beach, was named Lake Worth in his honor. The first road, the Military Trail, connecting the fort of Jupiter with Fort Dallas on Biscayne Bay, was forged through the junglelike hammocks and swamps. In 1845 the territory of Florida became the twenty-seventh state.

The Jupiter Lighthouse, the oldest structure in Palm Beach County, was built in 1859 as protection against the warlike Seminole Indians.

Pierce House, Hypoluxo Island, 1876.

The first settler of the island of Palm Beach was a reputed Civil War draft dodger who sought refuge in the Florida wilderness. A. O. Lang was a horticulturist, and his plantings of citrus, fig, mango, guava, and banana trees; frangipani, cactus, and poinsettia added greatly to the limited native foliage on the island. In 1867 another settler, Charles Moore, filed for the first homestead in the area, and this location later became the site of the first schoolhouse and church in the county. So, long after the Conestoga wagons had forced their way to the West, and men had tried their luck panning for gold in the streams of California, civilization was slowly trickling into Southern Florida.

By 1873 the population around Lake Worth numbered only eight. Captain William H. Moore and Captain H. D. Pierce and his family had moved to the area, and other permanent settlers came to the region later in the 1870s when blizzard-stricken families from the Middle West read articles about the charms of the inexpensive tropics.

Clearing the jungle growth from the land for farming was backbreaking work, and it was difficult for the Middle Western farmers to adjust to the tropical planting schedule, which they learned only by trial and error. They successfully grew sweet potato and pumpkin crops, and later tomatoes, peppers, and eggplant. Citrus crops flourished, but sugarcane and pineapples failed.

Game was plentiful in the woods, and the settlers killed bear, deer, possums, and wild turkey. In the winter season thousands of ducks flew over the lake. Often the Seminole Indians would appear with meat to trade. The first Christmas get-together for all the settlers around the lake was held in 1873 at the Moore house, where residents feasted on big possum, sweet potatoes, biscuits with cane syrup, and prickly pear pie.

The waters teemed with fresh- and saltwater fish and giant sea turtles. The season when the turtles came out of the sea to lay their eggs in the sand was an especially important time of year for the pioneers. Turtle eggs found buried on the beach were used for boiling and scrambling, pancakes, cakes, and breads. To balance the plenty of the land and sea, however, there were the ever-present dangers of panthers and alligators and the pestilence of mosquitoes, fleas, and red bugs that had lived undisturbed for so long in the swamps and jungles.

The biggest boon for the early settlers came in a different manner from the sea. The shipwrecks that occurred off the coast offered a veritable mail-order-catalogue selection as their cargoes floated to the beach. Beachcombers traded junk metal remnants of the frequent wrecks for necessary staples and supplies.

In 1878 the Spanish brig *Providencia*, with a cargo of 20,000 coconuts from Trinidad, was wrecked off the coast of Palm Beach near the present site of the Bath and Tennis Club. After salvaging the valuable nuts, the finders sold them to their neighbors for 2½ cents apiece. It was hoped that coconut plantations would produce the income-producing crop that the pioneers were looking for.

Life in the area during this early period was primitive, and constant toil and vigilance were necessary for survival. Homes were made of lumber washed onto the beach and had roofs of thatched palmetto fans that had to be replaced frequently.

Communication with the outside world was extremely difficult. The nearest town for purchasing supplies was 160 miles to the north, a trip that took from eight to twenty-one days. A letter sent from Palm Beach to Miami traveled 3,000 miles by rail and ship via New York and Cuba before delivery to the pioneer settlement to the south. This schedule was vastly improved with the initiation of a unique postal service known as the Barefoot Mailman, a carrier who walked the slipping sand beaches between Palm Beach and Miami in three days.

The small political and social life of the area centered around the Cocoanut* Grove Hotel, owned and operated by Mr. and Mrs. E. N. Dimick. Cap Dimick paid a dollar an acre for the lakefront property near today's Clarke Avenue. He offered transportation service to guests by meeting schooner passengers at Jupiter with his covered wagon. Pet alligators were kept in a small pool near the two-story hotel, and a path from the hotel and cottages had been hacked through the thick foliage to the beach. Everyone was warned to be armed, however, since wildcats were prevalent all over the island. It was at the Cocoanut Grove Hotel that the settlers on the lake had a Christmas gathering in 1880. Each family brought something for the feast held outside on the hotel grounds. That night the first dance was held in the hotel dining room, with music supplied by three members of the Brelsford family. Fifteen years

*Many early settlers erroneously added the letter "a" in spelling the word "coconut." This misspelling appears in many area names, e.g., Cocoanut Row.

4

Cocoanut Grove Hotel, the first hotel in Palm Beach, 1891.

later, this simple hotel structure would be destroyed by fire, and the nearby Cocoanut Grove Garden would be a rendezvous for the world's richest and most famous vacationers.

In 1885 a land rush began in the Lake Worth region, and homesteaders flocked to the area. The fourteen-mile-long island, bordered by Lake Worth and the Atlantic Ocean, no more than four blocks wide, still had no official name. In 1886 the approximately forty male residents of the island met and chose the name of Palm City for their community. Several weeks later the U. S. Post Office Department informed them that there already was a Palm City in Florida, and while the mail boat waited for their reply, Gus Ganford, George Lainhart, and E. M. Brelsford stood in the Brelsford store trying to decide on another name. Palm Beach was Ganford's suggestion, the other two agreed, and the town was officially named. It was a rugged, isolated, and unassuming settlement that was soon to receive the Midas touch of Florida's greatest builder, Henry Morrison Flagler.

Henry Morrison Flagler was a disciplined, self-made man who had become a millionaire as a partner in Standard Oil before falling in love with the state of Florida. Flagler made his first trip to Florida in 1878 when he and his wife came south for her health. His next trip was after his first wife's death and his marriage to her nurse. The couple took a belated honeymoon in St. Augustine, and it was during this trip that Flagler, with his great vision, began to make plans for the development of Florida. It was his dream to make the east coast of the state the rival of the European Riviera. He built a grand Spanish Renaissance hotel, the Ponce de Leon, in St. Augustine, and after its opening in 1888 it soon became a very fashionable winter resort of the wealthy. Another Flagler hotel was in Ormond Beach, south of St. Augustine, and still Flagler was anxious to investigate more of the southern coastline.

After making the arduous trip by steamer, Celestial Railroad (so named because it stops were Jupiter, Mars, Venus and Juno) and launch, he visited the area of Lake Worth in March, 1892. He was intrigued with the beauty of the island of Palm Beach, with its unique silhouette of the hundreds of graceful coconut palms. While North Florida had suffered several severe winters in the previous decade, the climate farther south was constantly mild. The land lay 1,400 miles farther south than the Riviera, 200 miles farther south than Cairo, and the warm waters of the Gulf Stream ran in close proximity to the island shore.

Flagler bought several tracts of land for the then exorbitant price of $75,000. Plans got under way immediately for the building of a hotel even more spectacular than the Ponce de León and for a railroad to bring the visitors to it. The hotel was completed in a record nine months, and on February 11, 1894, the Royal Poinciana opened with seventeen guests. After two subsequent additions, it became the largest wooden building in the world.

It was not, however, its physical immensity that made the Royal Poinciana such an important part of turn-of-the-century America, it was the opulent life-style that existed there for the wealthy—a way of life that quite probably will never be seen again in America. It was a curious mixture of simplicity and elegance.

Guests arrived by railroad for the season, which started right after Christmas. Many traveled in private railroad cars, great turn-of-the-century status symbols. Often there were over sixty of

The people waiting for the train in front of the Royal Poinciana Hotel on March 14, 1896, were identified as follows in the *Palm Beach Daily News Historical Number* published in 1936. Left to right: Colonel Philip M. Lydig, Miss Helen Morton (Mrs. Morton), Miss Gladys Vanderbilt (Countess Szechenyi), Miss Amy Townsend, Captain Rose, Mrs. Cornelius Vanderbilt, Miss Edith Bishop (Mrs. Moses Taylor), Miss Mabel Gerry (Mrs. Saxham Drury), Mr. Thomas Cushing, Mr. Edward Livingston, Mr. Dudley Winthrop, Mr. Craig Wadsworth, Miss Gertrude Vanderbilt (Mrs. Harry Payne Whitney), Mr. Lispenard Stewart, Mr. Harry Payne Whitney, Miss Sybil Sherman (Mrs. Stellar), Mr. Cornelius Vanderbilt. The Palm Beach Towers now rises where the old Royal Poinciana stood.

these palace cars lined up adjacent to the golf course. Passengers disembarked from the trains to be greeted by the courteous porters and bellmen, who somehow always managed to have the luggage waiting for the guests in their rooms by the time they had registered in the magnificent green and white lobby.

Because of the immediate popularity of the Royal Poinciana, in 1895 Flagler built the Palm Beach Inn on the ocean. It was later renamed the Breakers.

Many of the early guests at the Flagler hotels came south for their

7

The mule train that ran between the Royal Poinciana and the Breakers hotels was popular since Flagler permitted no horses or automobiles on the island.

health. There were so many visitors in poor health that native Floridians described anyone from north of Jacksonville as a "sick Yankee." But the hotel registers of those early times also contained the names of many who came for reasons other than health. Appearing on the register were the names of Harold S. Vanderbilt; the Duke and Duchess of Manchester; Mrs. George Jay Gould; Colonel John Astor; John W. "Bet-a-Million" Gates, the railroad tycoon; Henry C. Frick; Mr. and Mrs. John Wanamaker; Hugh Chisholm; and Senator Chauncey Depew.

The rooms at the Royal Poinciana contained the latest innovations. Each room had a telephone, electric lights, and the newest fire escape. For fire-safety devices, most buildings at this time offered only a long knotted rope with a hook on one end, but at the Royal Poinciana the fire escape had a galvanized fixture which released the rope. The user put the loop around his waist, held onto the rope, and was slowly lowered to the ground.

The splendid dining room could accommodate 1,600 people and

was staffed by 400 black waiters, one to each four diners, plus a headwaiter who had a secretary and twenty-six assistants. The tips were so big that one of the past headwaiters recollects that the waiters never had to touch their hotel pay until the end of the season. The hotel tips for the short season amounted to $250,000 each year.

It has been said that nowhere were the Gay Nineties gayer than in Palm Beach. The morning might start with a trip to the beach after breakfast. At the Breakers bathing casino a guest might choose to swim in the ocean or the pool while he was being serenaded by the combined orchestras of the two hotels. At the beach the bathing costume for ladies was strictly prescribed—black stockings that reached the bathing suit, with no skin showing.

The guests returned from the beach in time to change for a leisurely 1 P.M. luncheon. In the afternoon the men would play golf or tennis or fish; the ladies would sit on the porch and talk, play croquet, or ride in the Afromobiles (vehicles like large tricycles pedaled by blacks). Popular excursions were a drive up the lake trail to the Garden of Eden, a botanical wonder at the north end of the island, or perhaps a longer ride along the jungle trail to the south end to see the famous ocean wreck. A visit to Alligator Joe's to watch him wrestle the alligators at a site near the present Everglades Club was on everyone's list.

Royal Poinciana Hotel Grill Room.

Before the Bath and Tennis Club was formed, everyone swam at Gus' Baths.

Two guests in an Afromobile on Golf View Road.

Alligator Joe and his pets.

John W. Gates and his friends always came to Palm Beach for the shooting season at the gun club. Shooting expeditions into the Everglades and Big Cypress Swamp were popular. Hunters bagged wildcats and panthers as well as deer, wild turkey, and geese. The sport fishing was so good in those times that one afternoon John Pullman caught twenty-one amberjacks at the rate of one every eight minutes. That evening he was applauded by fellow guests in the lobby of the Royal Poinciana Hotel.

There were even more luxurious yachts than resplendent private Pullman cars. One of the most talked about belonged to Pierre Lorillard. He carried a small herd of Jerseys on board so that guests might have fresh milk at all times.

Everyone was sure to be back in time to change clothes for tea time at the Cocoanut Grove, located in the southwest corner of the hotel grounds. This was a lovely garden decorated with strings of bright lights where guests gathered at 5 P.M. to hear the latest rage, ragtime music. In between dances, guests would sample Mrs. Roche's famous coconut cake and a variety of beverages.

11

Royal Poinciana Hotel Lobby.

Tea in the afternoon in the Cocoanut Grove.

It was then time to change clothes again for dinner. A guest had several choices of where to dine in the evening. If he chose to stay in the hotel, he might select the main dining room or the Grill Room, where the groceries were imported from Park and Tilford in New York.

If it were a Thursday night, almost everyone would crowd into the hotel dining room, which had been cleared for the occasion in order to watch the Cake Walk. Ladies wore their best jewels and gowns to these important affairs. Cake Walks were so popular that they were often staged twice a week in the dining room and occasionally at tea time in the Cocoanut Grove as well. Six black couples, usually hotel employees, would take turns performing the dance. Flamboyantly dressed, they would strut and prance to the music of such popular songs as "In the Good Old Summertime," "Bill Bailey," "The Cake Walk Queen," and "Oh Dem Golden Slippers." The judges, always well-known hotel guests who included Frederick Vanderbilt and Admiral George Dewey, the hero of Manila Bay, awarded the prize money (sometimes as much as $500) and cake to the winners. That couple then danced around the floor holding the cake, and people were bound to say, "They take the cake!"

The end of the short season came on February 22 with the great social highlight of the year, the Washington's Birthday Ball. The typical menu would include consommé épicurien, salted almonds, olives, roast squabs, assorted sandwiches, boned capon with jelly, broiled quail with guava jelly, salads, Key West lobster, Neapolitan ice cream, punch, and assorted cakes.

The Washington's Birthday Ball was the official close of the season, and present-day natives still remember that the town would be full of visitors the day of the ball and empty the next. Many times the guests would leave the ball to retire to their private railroad cars, and by the time they awoke for breakfast they would be well on their return trip north. The season was over.

In all the thirty-seven years that the Royal Poinciana remained in operation, no guest ever saw the flowers of the beautiful flame trees for which the hotel was named. In the late spring and early summer, when the gorgeous royal poinciana trees burst forth with their red and orange showers of blooms, the hotel was deserted and quiet, waiting the start of the next season.

Colonel Bradley's Beach Club was within easy walking distance

Washington's Birthday Regatta on the grounds of the Brelsford House.

of both the Breakers and the Royal Poinciana hotels. The plain white clapboard building occupied the land that is now Bradley Park on the north side of Royal Poinciana Way at the lake. A bronze plaque marks the former site of the unpretentious building that was America's Monte Carlo.

Bradley's reputation was made from a well-run gambling operation, an excellent kitchen, and impeccable service. Conrad

Schmitt, one of Bradley's early chefs, was a Swiss with an international reputation. He introduced Bradley's patrons to green turtle soup at the then unbelievable price of $1 per serving. Turtles were paraded on a chain through the club before making their final trip to the soup pot. There was no bar at Bradley's. The Colonel did not encourage drinking in his establishment; drinks were available only at the dining tables. In the beginning there was no menu for dinner. The headwaiter made suggestions for food and wines, but prices were never mentioned. No one who belonged to Bradley's had to ask the price.

Bradley's acquired many devotees because of its food. A famous story is told of C. W. Barron, who founded *Barron's Weekly*. Barron considered Bradley's the best dining spot in the United States, and he was prepared to enjoy all of Chef Jean Broca's sumptuous food in comfort. When he came for the season, he brought tuxedos in five different sizes. As he continued to eat at Bradley's, he simply wore larger and larger clothes to fit his waistline. At the season's end, having graduated to his largest suit, he would depart for Saratoga Springs for a long session of weight-losing.

Bradley's was a private club, and Colonel Bradley was the entire membership committee. It is said that the two doormen at Bradley's recognized all the members immediately. Together they reportedly made $14,000 in tips each season. A nonmember was quickly stopped unless he was the guest of a member who had introduced his friend to the Colonel. All persons who were residents of the state of Florida, those who were not twenty-five years of age, or those who were even slightly intoxicated were immediately barred. Colonel Bradley was always in his office inside the main door to see that these rules were enforced. In the evenings after seven, gentlemen had to wear evening clothes; if not white tie and tails, then certainly a tuxedo.

The interior of Bradley's was not as lavish as might have been expected. The decor was green and white, with the green carpets matching the baize of the gambling tables. Colonel Bradley insisted on orange lights in the dining room so that the ladies in their magnificent jewels would look their best. After dinner, guests adjourned to the gambling rooms to try their luck. They could not bring their beverages with them since there was no drinking allowed in the gambling salon. Dignified demeanor was naturally expected of Colonel Bradley's guests.

A gold membership card to Bradley's was a highly prized

Bradley's Beach Club.

possession in Palm Beach. Most members were multimiliionaires or at least millionaires. It is said that Colonel Bradley was an astute judge of character and invited only those people he liked and thought could afford to gamble.

There are many stories about the disputes between Colonel Bradley and Henry Flagler. Because of his strict Presbyterian background, Flagler strenuously objected to women being allowed to gamble. He also worried about the effect of the gambling place on the town. It is reputed that at one point Flager tried to buy out Bradley for $350,000, but Bradley refused.

At Bradley's the stakes were high, and Colonel Bradley arbitrarily set the limits for each guest. He would walk around with a huge bankroll, personally paying off the big winners. House rules dictated that all debts had to be settled in twenty-four hours. It is said that some of the first-time big losers were invited by Bradley to pay their losses with a check for half their total debt. He had no desire to lose their business permanently.

In spite of the stories of the fabulous stakes, no attempt was ever made to rob Bradley's. Perhaps this was because it was also well known that Bradley protected the club with hidden riflemen, who were always on duty discreetly hidden behind decorative trellis-work. Thirty armed guards were also always on duty.

Another reason why Bradley's ran so smoothly for almost half a century was because of the care in the selection of the employees. All the dealers and croupiers were single men who lived in the barracks behind the Beach Club. If any married men were employed, their wives could not accompany them to Florida. The men were paid $20 to $50 a day plus room and board, and their pay was usually held for them until the end of the season—with a 10 percent bonus. There was no socializing with the patrons—this was grounds for immediate dismissal. On Sunday mornings Colonel Bradley would lead those of his men who were Catholics to church with him.

It was very seldom that Colonel Bradley was ever duped. One story of such an occurrence concerns a beautiful young woman who came to the Colonel one night and asked if she could speak to him privately in his office. She pointed through the glass doors at a man leaving the club and told Bradley tearfully that the man was her husband and that he had gambled away all the money they had in the world. Bradley agreed to refund the considerable su n of $5,000 provided that her husband never returned to the club again. The woman said she would make her husband agree to that stipulation, but requested that the Colonel let her handle the transaction since her husband would be embarrassed that she had appealed to Colonel Bradley. The Colonel agreed with her request. The next evening he was surprised to see the same young man at the tables again, and he promptly went to him to demand an explanation as to why he had returned. The man explained to the dumbfounded Colonel that he was in fact single and that he could certainly afford his losses. His family name was one of America's wealthiest. The Colonel never pressed charges or looked for the young woman, because he believed that anyone who had deceived him so successfully was entitled to the money.

Bradley's continued its successful operation for over forty years. Many years the Colonel's profits topped $1,000,000 a season. When Bradley died in 1946, his will provided that the club be torn down and the land donated to the Town of Palm Beach as a park, with the provision that nothing should be built there. One of the walls of the Colonel's private house is all that remains. Bradley's

Beach Club was an institution in Palm Beach and many would agree with what the late Joseph P. Kennedy said of Palm Beach after Bradley's closed: "The zipperoo has gone out of the place."

During the time that Henry Flagler was building the Royal Poinciana Hotel and beginning the development of Palm Beach, he was having serious personal problems. His only daughter, Jennie Louise, died in 1889 a few weeks after giving birth to a daughter, who lived only a few hours. His second wife was suffering from mental illness and was institutionalized late in 1897. Doctors gave him no hope for her recovery. In 1901 the Florida legislature passed a law which enabled a divorce to be granted on the grounds of insanity. His critics called it "Flagler's Divorce Law," and it was repealed four years later; but during the interim Flagler divorced his second wife and married for a third time. Flagler had met Mary Lily Kenan some ten years before while she was visiting relatives in St. Augustine. In August, 1901, the seventy-one-year-old Flagler married Mary Lily, who was then thirty-four, at her family home in North Carolina. His new bride wanted a "cottage in Palm Beach," and Whitehall was his wedding gift to her.

Flagler had told his architects, Carrère and Hastings, to build "the finest marble home you can think of." Whitehall, which cost $2,500,000 to build and $1,500,000 to furnish, was their answer. On the point of land that had once contained pioneer Palm Beach's first store and post office, a veritable American palace was raised in eighteen months.

The architecture of Whitehall shows a distinctly Spanish influence in the restrained elegance of its dazzling white exterior and its arrangement of the ground floor rooms around a central open court. This "Taj Mahal in the land of flowers," as the New York *Herald* referred to Whitehall, contained treasures which had been gathered by the Flaglers and their agents from all over the world, including the Vatican. Broad white marble steps lead to the wide, pillared porch that runs the length of the front of the building. Massive bronze doors open into the magnificent marble entrance hall, which is of seven shades of marble and topped with a large painting, "The Crowning of Knowledge," which was painted on canvas and then molded to the arched ceiling. Also on the first floor are exquisite gold and crystal chandeliers, priceless tapestries, antique Florentine chests, Boucher panels, and jeweled mirrors, as well as the largest Kirman rug ever loomed. A

Mary Lily Kenan Flagler in her wedding gown.

Whitehall, Henry Morrison Flagler's home—circa 1905.

Renaissance library paneled in Circassian walnut, a music room in the style of Louis XIV with the largest pipe organ ever placed in a private home, and a Swiss billiard room flank the south side of the central tropical court, and a French salon decorated in delicate colors and containing priceless furniture is on the north side of the Marble Hall. The salon opens into a formal dining room which contains twenty-four side and two arm chairs each covered in an individual Aubusson tapestry. The ceiling in this room is made of panels of antique ivory with gold relief. On the west side of the building is an enormous gold and ivory ballroom in Louis XV style. Flagler's designers thought of even the smallest details—in the ballroom the sconces contain crystal drops which are replicas of Florida fruits: avocados, guavas, and little Florida bananas.

On the second floor are sixteen guestrooms with private baths, which the Flaglers filled with the social, political, and financial leaders of the day. The Duke and Duchess of Manchester, John

The banquet room of Whitehall—circa 1902.

Astor, Admiral and Mrs. Dewey, Woodrow Wilson and Nellie (Dame) Melba were among those who came to enjoy the lavish Flagler hospitality, which seventeen servants helped him to maintain.

The papers of the time report that "the season started when the gates of Whitehall were opened!" This sign that Mr. and Mrs. Flagler were in residence usually occurred in the Christmas holidays. Mr. Flagler's birthday on January 2 was always celebrated with great pomp. Invitations to Whitehall were treasured, and for seveal years before ill-health came to the energetic tycoon, there was a fantastic swirl of activity during the three-month season. Music played an important part in the lives of both Mr. and Mrs. Flagler. They kept two organists in residence and enjoyed having them play for their guests. A guest such as Dame Melba would sing with the organ as accompaniment. Mary Lily Flagler had a pretty, trained voice, and sometimes would entertain with favorite selections. She often sang at meetings of the "Fortnightly Society," a group that met to share cultural experiences. The Flaglers entertained at "Sunset Teas" on the south porch after late-afternoon musical programs, and Mrs. Flagler had "at homes" on Thursday afternoons. Sometimes at these affairs rugs would be spread in the outdoor courtyard and tea would be served while a Neapolitan band played. Another popular entertainment was oyster roasts on the lawn, with a London palmist reading hands while the guests watched the motorboat races on the lake.

Besides these gala daytime activities, the Flaglers entertained elegantly in the evening at formal dinners and balls. One of the most famous was the "Millionaires' Dinner," which was a stag gathering for twenty guests in honor of the Honorable Julien T. Davies of New York. As the guests were enjoying their meal, served on the Italian gold service in the formal dining room lit by hundreds of candles, it occurred to someone that all these men from the world of finance, law, literature, drama, and the army had one thing in common—they were all millionaires!

The "Bal Poudre" at Whitehall in 1903 was heralded as "The most brilliant social event that has ever occurred in the Far South." Fourteen Palm Beach beauties dressed in white Colonial wigs adorned with wreaths of rosebuds started the first minuet of the Ball. Dancing was continued into the early morning while a fantastic supper was served before midnight. Favors for the guests

Henry Morrison Flagler and his wife, Mary Lily Kenan Flagler.

Henry Morrison Flagler entertaining ladies at tea on the lawn.

included miniature silver pots of cherry trees for the ladies and silver hatchets for the men. There were also souvenir silver loving cups with an engraving of Whitehall on the front.

Flagler spared no expense; he knew how much Mary Lily enjoyed this gala entertaining. Although he always carried his own lunch to his office and did not personally enjoy hard liquor, he made sure his guests had the best of everything. The chief cook at Whitehall was a woman whose cuisine was justifiably famous. Flagler ordered his staff to serve many tropical fruits, such as pineapples, to his Northern guests, who were unfamiliar with the delicacies. He wanted his guests to know and enjoy all the various aspects of the Florida life he loved so much.

Henry Flagler built one more thing in Palm Beach for Mary Lily after the completion of Whitehall. The railroad bridge crossed the lake just to the north of the mansion, and Mary Lily and her guests were bothered by the noise and the smoke from the engines that brought guests to the hotels. Flagler built a second bridge to the north of the Royal Poinciana Hotel and tore down the other.

At this point in his life Henry Morrison Flagler had one more goal: He wanted to continue his Florida East Coast Railroad from

Henry Morrison Flagler at the dock.

Miami to Key West. The railroad had reached the pioneer settlement of Miami, and the new town began to take shape immediately. Indeed, Flagler did so much for the development of the community that in 1896, when the town was incorporated, there was a popular move to name the city Flagler. Flagler declined this honor, however, and favored the colorful and appropriate Indian name of Miami.

From Miami he wanted his railroad to stretch on south through the chain of islands known as the Florida Keys to the city of Key West. The 156-mile route crossed hundreds of small keys, coral reefs, everglades, jungles, and broad expanses of sea. It took seven years, $20,000,000 and 3,000 men working continuously to complete his dream. The workers battled hurricanes, mosquitoes, and intense heat to complete the laying of the rails that for over half the distance were built over water or marshland on steel and concrete viaducts and bridges. Often during the building of the Key West extension, Mr. and Mrs. Flagler would take their Palm Beach guests in their private railroad car, the Rambler, down to the construction site. Many hailed the engineering feat as the eighth wonder of the world.

The first train pulled into the Key West Station on the morning of January 22, 1912, with Henry Flagler on board. The eighty-two-year-old pioneer declared in his brief speech, "Now I can die happy; my dream is fulfilled." Less than eighteen months later, on May 20, 1913, Henry Morrison Flagler died in Palm Beach.

After having spent over $50,000,000 in the development of Florida and establishing a generous trust for the maintenance of his second wife in a mental institution, Flagler's estate amounted to nearly $100,000,000. Most of this and the marble palace he had built for her went to Mary Lily.

For several years after Flagler's death Mary Lily kept Whitehall closed. In 1916 she married Robert Bingham and they opened Whitehall the following winter. One of the highlights of the 1916–17 season was their party for Mary Lily's niece, Louise Clisby Wise, who had made her debut that year in Wilmington. Louise Wise would inherit Whitehall when Mary Lily died in 1917.

The "war that would make the world safe for democracy" had little effect on the magical kingdom of Palm Beach.

The real revolution that was coming to Palm Beach was not a political one—it was one that would start with mortar and stone and end with changing the social structure of the town. No longer would Palm Beach be a "hotel society," for Addison Mizner and Paris Singer had come to Palm Beach.

Paris Singer arrived in Palm Beach in 1917 exhausted and ready to die. He was literally carried on a stretcher from the train to a small bungalow that he had rented on Chilean Avenue. Singer, who was named for the capital of France, was one of twenty-four children of Isaac Merit Singer of sewing machine fame. Most of these children were illegitimate, including Paris; but that fact did not prevent him from inheriting a large portion of his father's estate. Paris Singer was a true Renaissance man: handsome, blond, tall and full-bearded, he was an artist and an architect, a scholar, a patron of young poets and artists, an athlete, a scientist, a philanthropist, and friend of royalty.

He was also known as quite a lover, and his tempestuous affair with the dancer Isadora Duncan flared again and again in many countries during the decade it lasted. Singer came to Palm Beach, worn out by the war in Europe and by his skirmishes with the volcanic Isadora, to finish his days alone in peace and sunshine.

In 1918 another invalid came to Palm Beach for his health. Addison Mizner, at age forty-five, had just escaped financial bankruptcy and was suffering severe emotional stress. In addition to this he was suffering acute physical pain in his leg from complications of a boyhood injury. His past life had been filled with diverse and flamboyant experiences and careers. He was enervated.

Mizner was born in Benicia, California, the sixth of seven children of one of the oldest and most respected families in California. In 1889 his father, Lansing Bond Mizner, was appointed by Benjamin Harrison as envoy extraordinary and minister plenipotentiary to five countries in Central America. Leaving the rest of the family at home, he departed for Guatemala City with Addison, then seventeen, and his younger brother Wilson.

Life was never really the same for Addison and Wilson after their experience in Guatemala. The brothers shared a Spanish valet and tutor and developed an extraordinary taste for both the high and low life. A young priest who was a friend of Addison interested him in Spanish art and architecture, an enthusiasm that would last a lifetime. When Addison returned to California, the weaknesses in his academic preparation were very obvious, and there was no chance of his attending the University of California. His parents sent him instead to study at a university in Spain for a few months, and in later life he found that "educated at the University of Salamanca" opened many doors for him. A subsequent trip to China provided him with several chow dogs and a love for Chinese art and pajamas.

On Mizner's twenty-first birthday his father died, leaving the family proud but poor. Mizner was working for an architect, Willis Polk, known as the father of the American bungalow. Under the guidance of Polk, Mizner picked up some knowledge of architecture, but he never learned to draw detailed plans or write a set of specifications. But as his biographer, Alva Johnston, points out in *The Legendary Mizners,* Addison "was saved from being a dilettante by a genuine love of toil and saved from being a complete snob by his admiration for anybody who could do good work with his hands."

Mizner's career as an architect in San Francisco came to an abrupt halt because of the demands of his creditors. He roamed about the Klondike and the Pacific, selling antiques, prizefighting in Australia, finally turning to the literary life.

He returned to San Francisco a new kind of hero. A book he had written in collaboration with Ethel Mumford, *The Cynic's Calendar,* a collection of debauched proverbs, had caught the fancy of the American public and left it laughing. "The wages of gin is breath"; "Where there's a will, there's a lawsuit." These and other witticisms made him a new celebrity. However, royalties on the book were insufficient to support his life-style, and he returned to Guatemala with dreams of becoming a coffee king. There he found a new avocation, and in his own words he became "the greatest cathedral looter in the world." Because of the impoverished state of the Church, many religious establishments in Guatemala lay in ruins. Mizner bought stacks of religious vestments and altar cloths, crucifixes, altars, and paintings. He recounted later that he would never start bargaining by offering more than 1 percent of the value of the article he wanted to buy.

Returning in 1904 to New York with his ecclesiastical plunder, he quickly became the darling of society. Some of his former friends from San Francisco days were now enthroned in New York's "400." One of these, Mrs. Hermann Oelrichs, helped establish him in a shop on Fifth Avenue, and religious vestments used as wall decorations and piano throws became quite the vogue. Mizner had a coterie of friends in New York that included social leaders, business tycoons, and opera and theater stars. He was well liked by all for his penetrating wit and outlandish comments. He was something of a celebrity, walking his chows on Fifth Avenue, his 250 pounds clad in Chinese silk pajamas.

Mizner moved to Long Island in order to have the proper setting to display his collection of animals and memorabilia. He did a small business as a landscape architect specializing in Japanese gardens; however, he was always just one step in front of the creditors. His mother's death in 1915 was a great blow to him and his brother Wilson. The advent of World War I brought an end to his architectural commissions and, with bad health a serious problem, he decided to return to Guatemala to wait for the end of his days. Friends persuaded him to visit Palm Beach instead.

After recuperating in the healthy climate of Palm Beach, neither Singer nor Mizner was content to die, but both were bored. A story is told that one day the two were sitting on the porch of the Royal Poinciana Hotel when Paris Singer asked Addison Mizner what he would do if he could do anything he wished. Mizner looked around the Royal Poinciana and saw in the distance the Breakers and several frame cottages. "I'll tell you what I'd do. I'd build something that wasn't made of wood, and I wouldn't paint it yellow!"

A great combination was formed—Addison's ideas and Singer's money. Singer had already given one of his elaborate English

Left to right—Addison Mizner, Marie Calhoun, Mrs. Paris Singer, and Paris Singer.

estates and donated money for the establishment of convalescent homes for the Allied soldiers in England and France. He wanted to contribute further to the war effort and made the statement to friends, "My wealth came from this country, yet I have never shown any appreciation in return. It seems to me that Palm Beach would be an ideal location for a convalescent hospital for officers." Singer commissioned Addison Mizner to design this convalescent home, and he bargained to buy eighty acres of real estate near Alligator Joe's farm. When he received the papers he found that the owner had included twice the agreed-on acreage at the same cost. At first he was reluctant to accept the proposition, as he would have the expense of clearing the land, killing the rattle-snakes, and paying the additional taxes. After some hesitation he decided to accept all 160 acres, and this site is the present Everglades Club on Worth Avenue and its golf course.

Meanwhile Singer had given Mizner carte blanche in his plans for the convalescent hospital. Somehow Mizner's misspent life seemed to be the perfect preparation for this new career in which he found himself.

The plans for the building grew more grandiose the longer they were on the drawing board. What began to emerge was more an Alhambra than a hospital. For twenty years Paris Singer had made a hobby of collecting old tiles from ruined buildings around the Mediterranean. These antique tiles Mizner used in decorating pavements, fountains, and galleries. Years later a group of Tunisians entered the building and immediately assumed positions of worship before the collection of tiles that had been salvaged from an ancient Tunisian mosque.

Because of the war there was a scarcity of building materials, so Mizner was forced to improvise. He trained local workmen to develop the skills that his designs called for—a local blacksmith became an expert in wrought iron, and a West Palm Beach painting contractor was taught the intricacies of making ornamental cast stone. Later, his own workshops produced the ceramic tiles that he used lavishly.

Paris Singer sent out over 300,000 invitations to veterans to come to Palm Beach at his expense. To his astonishment he received only thirty-three replies. The war had ended and the need for a military hospital had lessened. His wealthy friends convinced him that they needed a private club to escape the bourgeois guests at the

Three interior views of the Everglades Club.

hotels. So in 1919, the Mizner-designed convalescent hospital became the Everglades Club with Paris Singer the sole owner. It quickly became the focal point of Palm Beach society, and Singer became the social dictator of the town. Club membership cards were issued for one year only, and an invitation to return the following year was dependent wholly on Paris' likes or dislikes. He capriciously kept one woman out because she laughed too loudly. His escapades with Isadora were a thing of the past, and he was shocked if any scandal touched his members. Someone suggested to him that Colonel Bradley be admitted as a member, but Singer was outraged that a "professional gambler" was considered. He also was adamant in refusing anyone "in trade" or commercial business. After dusk, formal evening clothes were required, though the eclectic Singer himself spent his days in a Basque beret, purple espadrilles, and the wide-striped trousers favored by Europeans. He ran the club according to his own personal whims.

The opening of the club was a gala affair with one fatal flaw. Since war precluded furnishing the club with authentic antiques, Mizner had made his own Spanish furniture, using quicklime and shellac to antique the leather on the chairs. They looked lovely, but when the beautifully gowned ladies sat on them on opening night, the heat from their bodies and the quicklime softened the shellac, and they were literally stuck. Mizner spent much of the night pulling distraught females from their chairs. The next morning swatches of material stuck to the shellac testified as to who had sat where.

At first many of the members thought that the beautiful new club was in the wilderness. They were used to the convenience of Bradley's and the hotels. Singer started Thursday-night soirées, which became quite popular, and then he initiated Sunday evenings also. He was a charming host on these occasions, but apparently whenever he decided that it was time for everyone to leave, he would extinguish the lights in the club.

As the club increased in popularity, Mizner built the maisonettes on the east side flanking Worth Avenue. There were shops on the ground floor and town houses above, overlooking the tennis courts.

All of Palm Beach was fascinated with Addison Mizner after the unveiling of the Everglades Club. One of those who was most impressed was Mrs. E. T. Stotesbury, "Queen Eva," who held

Mrs. Eva Stotesbury.

sway over Palm Beach society with an iron hand in a velvet glove during the 1920s and 1930s.

Mr. E. T. Stotesbury was a Philadelphian who had made his fortune in banking. Starting as a grocery clerk, he later became associated with Drexel and Company and worked his way up to head the company. He was also a partner of J. P. Morgan. The Stotesburys were married late in life. Mrs. Stotesbury was a widow and Stotesbury was sixty-three, but their hectic life-style belied Mr. Stotesbury's advanced age.

In 1916 she had built a 154-room mansion in Whitemarsh outside Philadelphia and was just beginning to work with the architect on a set of plans for a home in Palm Beach when she saw the Everglades Club.

She decided that she must have a Mizner house. El Mirasol, view of the sun, was the result. It is said that the building started out to look like a Spanish convent and ended up looking like a Spanish castle. Mizner was so interested in the forty-car underground garage that he completely forgot the kitchen until someone brought the oversight to his attention. Mrs. Stotesbury would often say in later years that the house had genuine fifteenth-century plumbing.

The grounds of El Mirasol stretched from the ocean to the lake, bordered by Wells Road to the south. Renowned for the spectacular landscaping, it had a private zoo, at least half a dozen patios, a pool with underwater lighting, and a teahouse overlooking the lake. This was reputed to be the spot where Ponce de Leon landed

Fountain at El Mirasol, the Stotesbury residence.

Mr. Edward T. Stotesbury's yacht *Nedeva*.

when he visited Palm Beach four centuries before. The house itself
contained thirty-seven rooms including a sunroom auditorium
and a reception room for the chauffeurs of the Stotesburys' guests.
Fifty servants maintained the estate. Mrs. Stotesbury's grandson,
who still lives in Palm Beach, remembers that the security guards
were former White Russian soldiers who wore their uniforms and
decorations while patrolling the grounds.

Mr. Stotesbury's birthday party on February 26 rivaled the
Washington's Birthday Ball as the highlight of the season. Originally it was a luncheon party, but on Mr. Stotesbury's seventy-
sixth birthday it was changed to a musical and tea from 5 to 7 P.M.
Five hundred guests were invited and a name orchestra was
brought from the North. At his eightieth celebration Mr. Stotesbury was found watching the drummer in silent fascination.
Someone gave him a pair of drumsticks, and he played continu-
ously for the next fifteen minutes, demonstating the skill that he
had employed years before as a drummer in the Union Army
during the Civil War. For the next nine years Mr. Stotesbury's
playing the drums at his birthday party became a tradition.

The Stotesburys entertained elaborately all during the season, filling the mansion with houseguests who, on arising, would select their meals for the day from menus by Cartier. Mr. Stotesbury is said to have attempted to keep the weekly Palm Beach expenses at $12,500.

El Mirasol was also the setting for recitals, benefits, and lectures by distinguished speakers. During one piano recital Addison Mizner lured Mr. Stotesbury away for a quick game of pinochle. Mrs. Stotesbury discovered them in one of the patios and chastised Addison, "You sneak away while Rachmaninoff is playing." Mizner lowered his head and replied, "Oh, I thought it was the piano tuner."

Mrs. Stotesbury's jewel collection was considered to be one of the most impressive in the world. Among other pieces she owned a diamond necklace worth over $1,000,000, given to her by J. P. Morgan as a wedding present, a diamond and sapphire necklace from her husband, and a priceless strand of pearls. Mr. Stotesbury seldom wore more than a stickpin, but he loved to see his wife ablaze with jewels.

Mrs. Stotesbury had three children by her first marriage, and one of her sons, James Cromwell, married two of the wealthiest women in the country, Delphine Dodge and Doris Duke. In 1922 Mrs. Stotesbury's daughter, Louise, married General Douglas MacArthur at El Mirasol, and even though the marriage ended in divorce, Mrs. Stotesbury always remained a close friend of the General's.

When Mrs. Stotesbury died in 1946, the Lake Worth *Herald* reported that her passing could epitomize the end of the era of splendid mansions in Palm Beach.

The Mizneresque Palm Beach style has been variously described as Moorish, Romanesque, Gothic, Renaissance, and Spanish. One of America's ambassadors to Spain, while visiting in Palm Beach, called it "more Spanish than anything in Spain." But whatever name one assigns to the style, Addison Mizner, architect without formal training, was transforming Palm Beach into a medieval city. One critic compared him to Michelangelo and the builders of the Acropolis. Frank Lloyd Wright, who thought little of all the public buildings in Washington, heaped great praise on Mizner. There was one thing that Mizner understood perfectly—his wealthy

The Stotesbury-MacArthur wedding.

Playa Riente, the residence of first Mr. and Mrs. Joshua Cosden, later Mrs. Horace Dodge.

clients wanted their Palm Beach homes to reflect their riches and their prestige. The opulence of their residences was a measure of their social position.

Playa Reinte was one of the most spectacular homes that Mizner ever built. It was constructed in 1923 on the ocean north of the Palm Beach Country Club for multimillionaire oil man Joshua Cosden at a cost of $1,800,000. One of its outstanding features was a ballroom built out over the ocean and decorated with nine gigantic paintings by José Sert. The mural depicted the Arabian nights adventures of Sinbad, and the paint was mixed with gold and silver dust to create the impression of light emanating from the scenes themselves.

Cosden was a charming man who had started out as a streetcar conductor in Baltimore. Owning one of the largest Mizner houses in Palm Beach greatly aided the Cosdens in their climb up the social ladder. Discovering that entertaining nobility was one of the keys to immediate social success, he and his wife invited the Prince of Wales, Lord Mountbatten, and others. In their rivalry the Cosdens and the Stotesburys entered into a battle of patios, and called on Mizner to enlarge their homes. After several additions, El Mirasol was definitely larger than Playa Reinte, and "Queen Eva" Stotesbury remained the reigning monarch of Palm Beach.

Two years after building their house the Cosdens sold the estate at a profit of $1,000,000 to Mr. and Mrs. Hugh Dillman. Mrs. Dillman, who was later to return to her former name of Mrs. Horace Dodge, loved to entertain in the magnificent house, and she did it in a very formal way. She favored large cocktail parties and would feature huge bowls of caviar. Like Mrs. Stotesbury, Mrs. Dodge had a remarkable collection of jewelry. Her prize piece was a strand of pearls that had belonged to Russia's Catharine the Great. If the ropes of pearls had been unwound, they would have made a string as long as Mrs. Dodge was tall. Mrs. Dodge loved to travel, and she had a grand yacht, the *Delphine,* named for her daughter. It had a crew of forty-three and featured a large pipe organ which could disappear. She intrigued her guests by asking them to take turns ordering all the meals on a given day.

It was a mark of privilege to have a Mizner house with a part missing. Mizner was having a wonderful time building a home for George Rasmussen at 780 South Ocean Boulevard when the owner questioned the lack of a staircase between the first and second floor. Mizner insisted that an indoor staircase would spoil his design, so he added a turret with outdoor wrought-iron stairs. Later, in designing the Boca Raton Club, Mizner added a lovely arched doorway that opened into the back of a chimney. He liked to modify his plans when he became inspired during construction, and paid no heed to the cost of changing an almost completed building. He wanted his houses to look as if they had developed over the centuries, and he believed that construction came first and blueprints followed.

Mizner's unorthodox manner of giving the kiss of centuries to his creations was the despair of his workmen. He would take the hammer to newly constructed statues and mantelpieces. He would burn tarpaper in a freshly painted room in order to soften the colors and make them look centuries older. His men would be instructed to spray condensed milk on newly painted frescoes and then wipe down the walls with steel wool. Worm-eaten timbers for ceilings were his favorite, but if he ran short of these, he used pecky cypress, filling the holes with paint pigments and then scraping them out again. Anything to achieve the effect of deteriorated magnificence—this was his creed.

In 1925, at the peak of his activity, Mizner was working on hundreds of houses and had turned down at least that many more commissions. Unfortunately some of his most famous homes, such as El Mirasol and Playa Reinte, have been demolished and the land subdivided. One of the most recent demolitions was that of Casa Bendita, the Phipps estate off North County Road near the Stotesbury estate. The present roads named Casa Bendita and El Mirasol mark the settings of the former elegant Mizner homes. Other famous Mizner homes in the area include Charles Munn's Amado; the late Arthur Hammerstein's Casa Ondrio on Seaspray Avenue; Colonel Anthony R. Kuser's Los Incas near Casa Bendita, now the residence of Mr. and Mrs. Stephen Sanford; and the Rodman Wanamaker house on North Ocean Boulevard, which for many years has been the home of the Joseph P. Kennedy family.

Mizner built himself a magnificent apartment located on top of a shopping center. He designed nineteen buildings that would house forty small shops, all on different levels, so that from the top floors of his tower the complex looked like a Mediterranean hilltop town. Mizner's tower was the archbishop's palace that overlooked all the activity. Located almost directly across the street from the Everglades Club, he built a bridge to link his apartment with his architectural offices, and the small alley underneath became the Via Mizner. His five-story apartment contains a forty-by-forty living room with a twenty-foot ceiling which he furnished with priceless Spanish antiques. In the dining room he installed the original paneling from a chamber at the University of Salamanca in which Christopher Columbus supposedly was commissioned by Queen Isabella. Mizner found that his friends and patrons were so impressed with the history of this paneling that he developed a method to copy wood paneling, and a dozen reproductions are found in Palm Beach homes.

Mizner created excitement wherever he went because of his immense size; his weight soared to over 300 pounds. He wore eccentric outfits, usually with his shirttails flying in the wind. He was generally accompanied by his two chows, a macaw, and two monkeys. At one time he owned two anteaters. One of the monkeys, Johnny Brown, was his constant companion, wrapped around his neck wherever he went. When Johnny died, Mizner buried him in the Via Mizner with a tombstone reading JOHNNY BROWN—THE HUMAN MONKEY.

When Paris Singer returned in 1925 from a trip to Europe, he was most displeased to think that the architect whom he had originally financed was building a project with the name Via Mizner. The two had a falling out over the undertaking, and the next year, on Singer's land adjacent to the Via Mizner, a new group of shops appeared in the Via Parigi.

Adding to the breakdown in the Mizner-Singer partnership was the arrival in town of Addison's brother Wilson. Wilson, the youngest and the scapegrace of the Mizner family, was everything that Paris Singer disliked. Wilson had been a con man, a cardshark, and a hustler along with a short career as a legitimate playwright.

Addison installed him as the manager of his tile workshop in an attempt to rehabilitate him. Wilson took over the management in a spectacular way. Most of the workshop laborers were blacks, and Wilson discovered they had wonderful voices. Every day for an hour or two he would bring in a portable organ and train the Mizner choir.

The ground swells of the Florida boom had been building up in 1922 and 1923, and by 1924 and 1925 the tidal wave of the biggest boom this country has ever known came to South Florida. Palm Beachers had not jumped into the boom at the beginning, but when enormous profits were made on the resale of Palm Beach estates, the fever spread. During 1924 and 1925 the Mizner brothers were temporarily multimillionaires while the money poured in from their work in Palm Beach and from the sale of lots in their new subdivision, Boca Raton, about thirty miles south.

However, there were ominous signs on the horizon that the bubble was about to burst. In the late fall of 1925 the second payments fell due on thousands of properties. Many who had bought these properties had gambled that they would be able to sell them at an exorbitant profit before the second payment became due. Now they were thrown on the real estate market in a desperate attempt to raise cash. In January, 1926, a headline in *Variety* read FLORIDA SLIPPING, and the craze to sell was on. The bubble had burst. There were literally thousands of lawsuits, and the Mizners were frequently sued. Wilson stayed in Palm Beach until 1927, when he left for California; Addison, however, attempted to stand behind Boca Raton until the end. He assumed the personal responsibility for the company's debts and this was to ruin him financially.

In the twenties, for those who weren't busy building homes or moving into grand estates, hotel life at the Royal Poinciana and the Breakers continued at a gay pace. In the morning guests flocked to the beach to swim and sunbathe or stroll and be photographed for the Northern newspapers.

The Cocoanut Grove at the Royal Poinciana was still the place to go in the late afternoon to listen to the music of Lucky Roberts or Broadway Jones while sipping gin and orange juice or a rum drink. Mrs. Roche's coconut cake was still a favorite for tea. After dinner there was dancing, a Cake Walk, or a trip to Bradley's or the Everglades Club. The tropical winter evenings were cool, and women did not hesitate to wear their full-length mink coats and long ermine capes. Their gowns and jewels were elaborate, and Dolly Martin is remembered parading down the Poinciana's Peacock Alley with genuine diamonds in the heels of her shoes.

In the private railroad cars by the fourteenth green of the Breakers Golf Course there were frequent men's gatherings at which enormous sums of money would exchange hands. The story is told that one night Joshua Cosden, J. Leonard Replogle, J. P. Donahue, Harry "Earl" Sinclair, Harry Doheny (of the Tea Pot Dome Scandal), and E. B. McLean were having a friendly game of poker. New York banker Morty Schiff joined the group and asked what they were playing. "Ten-thousand-dollar table stakes," someone murmured. "Count me in," said Schiff, and they threw him one chip.

Interest in sporting activities was increasing, and more and more men enjoyed golfing on the two local courses. There were two well-publicized tournaments, the Lake Worth Championship, first held in 1928, and the South Florida Championship, both played on the golf course located between the Breakers and the Royal Poinciana. Rather than grass greens this course had carefully maintained sand "greens." As players approached one of these greens, an employee would leap from his station under a nearby palm and prepare the surface by dragging a piece of carpet behind him back and forth over the sand.

The other local course, called the Palm Beach Country Club, had true grass greens. This course, which is still called by the same name, was organized as a private club in 1953 under the leadership of Morris Brown, who served as its first president. Its charter members included Joseph P. Kennedy, who often played golf on the links near his northend home. John F. Kennedy was a honorary member who also enjoyed the course.

Tennis attracted many players and spectators. There was always activity at the eight courts at the Royal Poinciana with George Agutter, the pro from Forest Hills, overseeing the play. Other courts were at the Everglades Club and the Seaspray Beach Club. In addition to the interclub competition, there were two major seasonal tournaments, the Men's Florida Championship and the Women's Florida Championship, played at the Royal Poinciana courts. One of Palm Beach's ranking tennis players was Arthur Hammerstein.

Many Palm Beach parties were planned with a theme, and costume parties were especially popular. There were pajama parties, shipwreck parties, barn parties, and in the later years of the decade, hard-times parties. One Palm Beach hostess asked her guests to come dressed as their theme songs; the orchestra played each song as the guest entered the room. An innovative lady, capitalizing on the current backgammon fad, gave a "Human Backgammon" party. A large canvas approximately forty-eight

Mrs. Raymond P. Baker (the former Mrs. Alfred Gwynne Vanderbilt) tees off a toe at the Everglades Club.

feet square was painted as a backgammon board and laid on the patio. Two oversize dice were made which were rolled by two opposing players. The women served as red makers and the gentlemen as black. With each roll of the dice the players directed their human markers to move around the game board. The "Human Backgammon Game" drew many letters from all parts of the country when it was written up in the society columns.

Catastrophe struck Palm Beach when the Breakers Hotel burned to the ground March 18, 1925. This was the third time that the Breakers had been ravaged by fire. Originally built as the Palm Beach Inn in 1895, the hotel was being enlarged in 1903 when a disastrous fire destroyed it. Henry Flagler ordered it rebuilt immediately, and the new structure was almost completed when fire again leveled the building. It finally reopened in 1904 as the Breakers Hotel.

The Breakers had approximately 450 guests in residence that day in 1925 when fire broke out. Mrs. Edward F. Hutton and Miss Billie Burke were talking to the desk clerk when a woman slipped in and whispered to the clerk that she had seen billows of yellow smoke coming from the top floor. Hotel employees tried to contain the

The Breakers' fire.

Aftermath of The Breakers' fire.

blaze, but it was soon out of control. Two fire departments in Palm Beach answered the alarm; then calls went out to West Palm Beach, Lake Worth, and even Miami.

Since it was the middle of the day, most of the guests at the Breakers were out of the hotel building and first learned of the fire when they heard the engines and the loud popping sound that the fire gave off. Crowds huddled on the grounds of the hotel, watching the inferno. It took only two hours for the four-story walls to cave in, and all the while the sparks were flying over the area. It was such a spectacular scene that ship captains brought their vessels in close to shore so that the passengers could watch.

The Palm Beach Hotel, located north of Bradley's on the lakefront, caught fire from the flying embers. One life was lost in this fire, and the damage to both hotels ran into the millions. Fortunately, a new hospital had opened, the first in the area, and the Good Samaritan in West Palm Beach aided the injured. One thousand homeless fire victims were taken into the Royal Poinciana Hotel.

Joe Risden, who owned a famous restaurant on Main Street (now Royal Poinciana Way), remembered seeing the lawn strewn with mink coats and steamer trunks that had been thrown from the hotel windows and abandoned in the excitement. Most of the guests lost all the belongings in their rooms, and when the hotel

Palm Beach Hotel, facing Lake Worth.

vault was finally opened days later, they found that some of the jewelry had melted in the intense heat.

Newspaper accounts of the town during the week following the blaze reported that the main streets were heavily patrolled to guard against looting and that "cars were courteously searched."

It would seem that with all the excitement about the fire, everyone in town was there to watch the Breakers go down. There were thousands of spectators. It has been recorded, however, that several stalwart golfers continued playing their round of golf—while their possessions burned.

In 1926 Addison and Wilson Mizner, like hundreds of developers in Miami, knew that the Florida bubble had burst. Those who had speculated in Florida land had little more than worthless pieces of paper to show for their millions of dollars of investment. In Palm Beach, however, life continued much as before.

As the reputation of the resort spread, there was a demand for more hotel rooms, and after the burning of the Breakers and the Palm Beach Hotel, three new hotels opened during 1926—the Whitehall, the Alba, and the new Breakers.

Whitehall was a luxury hotel opened on the grounds of Henry Flagler's home. After Flagler's widow, Mary Lily, died in 1917,

Whitehall was left to Mary Lily's niece, Louise Clisby Wise. Louise soon married Lawrence Lewis, but the newly married couple chose not to live in Whitehall, and they opened the mansion only once in February of 1924 for a lavish ball given with a cousin, Colonel Owen Kenan. *Palm Beach Life* called the ball "one of the most brilliant and dazzling balls of the season."

A month later the papers announced that Whitehall had been sold. Plans to turn the magnificent mansion into an exclusive club were never completed, and the owners decided instead to make it a luxury hotel by adding an eleven-story tower containing 300 rooms. One of the most elaborate suites in the new hotel was a grand penthouse offering a striking view of both the Atlantic Ocean and Lake Worth. The formal opening of Whitehall in January, 1926, drew large crowds of guests—so many that many diners had to be turned away. Dance music was supplied by John Philip Sousa III, who made his debut as an orchestra leader that night.

Whitehall was unique as a hotel in that it offered both the grandeur of the Flagler mansion and the convenience of the new tower. The hotel dining room seated 500 comfortably, and Flagler's original dining room was available for private entertaining. The Palm Court of Whitehall with its stately potted palms was a favorite meeting place for hotel guests and members of the cottage colony. There were dinner dances every Wednesday and Saturday nights during the season, and the Meyer Davis orchestra was the attraction of the 1927–28 season.

The hotel continued in operation until 1959, when it was purchased by The Henry Morrison Flagler Museum, restored as it was in Flagler's day. Jean Flagler Matthews, granddaughter of Henry Flagler, was the guiding personality in the establishment of the Museum as a memorial to her grandfather and as an addition to the cultural life of Palm Beach.

Palm Beach in the twenties was awash with titles. It seemed as though every European royal family had sent representatives to the resort.

It seemed natural then that when Maurice Heckscher was building his new hotel he should choose to name the establishment The Alba after a Spanish duke. The 550-room hotel designed by William Treanor and Maurice Fatio was built during 1925 and 1926 for an estimated $7,000,000. Another $2,000,000 was spent to furnish it. It was built around a Spanish courtyard and one of its well-publicized features was an elaborate suite of rooms where the Duke of Alba was to stay. The suite included a series of salons and galleries, a dining hall, and five bedrooms.

The grand opening was planned for February, and the town was buzzing with excitement about the party in honor of the Duke of Alba when the news came to the owner that the Duke was ill and would not be able to make the trip from Europe. The owner would not give up his plan at this stage and hired an actor to impersonate the Duke. The night of the party found the bellmen resplendent in uniforms sporting the Alba crest, the waiters dressed in Spanish costumes, and the cream of Palm Beach society enjoying the entertainment and free-flowing champagne. The masquerading actor was charming as the Duke. However, as the festivities wore on, his accent faltered, his makeup ran, he swayed under his heavy robes, and the secret of the ruse was out.

The Alba closed in 1929 and has since operated as The Ambassador Hotel, a naval convalescent hospital, and finally as The Biltmore Hotel. Currently, the building is unoccupied and its future is undecided.

The new Breakers was opened for guests on December 29, 1926. Its architectural style is modified Spanish with Italian Renaissance accents, with twin towers and graceful arches inspired by the Villa Medici in Rome. It stands today as a bastion of past elegance which cost six million dollars to build.

The present hotel contains much of the grace and charm of the Old World. The spacious lobby with its vaulted ceilings and frescos, the elaborate ceiling in the Gold Room, and the hand-painted beamed ceiling in the Florentine dining room reflect the artistry of the Italian Renaissance. Even the fountain in the front of the hotel is patterned after the one in the Boboli Gardens in Florence.

During the twenties and thirties the Venetian Lounge was the scene of many luncheons and bridge parties, and the seaside terrace was a favorite spot for tea-dancing at the sunset hour. Orchestras such as Howard Lanin's played for dancers after 9 P.M. It was the only hotel in Palm Beach offering a dance floor overlooking the ocean, and its Grand Loggia was the site of a yearly costume party for children.

The Breakers Hotel.

The Breakers' Dining Room.

The Breakers' Dining Room.

The reputation of the old Breakers brought back many of the guests who had enjoyed the hotel before the fire, and the beauty of the new hotel attracted many new visitors. The register of the Breakers during those years shows such names as John D. and William Rockefeller, Stephen Harkness, John Jacob Astor, J. P. Morgan, President Harding, William Randolph Hearst, Nellie Melba, William K. Vanderbilt, the Duchess of Marlborough, and Andrew Mellon.

The hotel, renovated and expanded in 1969, has lengthened its short operating season to be open year around, and is the only reminder of the hotel boom of the twenties.

Many of the private clubs in Palm Beach were founded during the twenties when members of the cottage colony wanted places other than the hotels to meet and relax. Much of the social activity in the town today takes place in these clubs, and the visitor who comes expecting to find a Miami-like night life will be sadly disappointed at the conservative aspect of the resort.

Bradley's Beach Club and the Everglades Club were prospering when a group under the leadership of Edward F. Hutton and A. J. Drexel Biddle decided that there was need for a family club where members and their children could swim and play tennis. The Bath and Tennis club, located on South Ocean Boulevard at Southern Boulevard, was founded to meet these needs. The semi-Moorish building was designed by Joseph Urban and the construction cost was over $1,000,000. It opened for the 1926–27 season, and the *Palm Beach* Daily News reported, "The elite of Palm Beach society here who are included in the membership list of the organization will paddle in the surf to the strains of Meyer Davis' orchestra which has been engaged for the season." The club also featured special tennis exhibition matches before lunch was served "beach style" on paper plates.

The founder memberships, which cost $10,000 each, were subscribed to quickly and the secretary sent back over $250,000 in checks after the quota had been filled. Some of the founder-members were Mr. and Mrs. E. T. Stotesbury, Walter Chrysler, Harry Payne Bingham, Mr. and Mrs. Chester Bolton, Colonel Edward R. Bradley, Lammot duPont, John Pillsbury, Herbert Pulitzer, Mrs. Isabel Dodge Sloan, Charles C. Woolworth, and Mrs. James P. Donahue. A. J. Drexel Biddle was the first president of the club, and Harris Hammond and Edward F. Hutton were the first vice-presidents.

Two important golf clubs came into being in the twenties. The Gulf Stream Golf Club, for men only, was organized in 1924. Its Mizner clubhouse is located in Delray Beach and apparently some of the members felt that its distance from Palm Beach was a real asset since they could get away from the ladies for several hours at a time. The Gulf Stream Golf Club boasts a $1,000,000 eighteenth hole since members voted not to sell a strip of their oceanfront property for $1,000,000 just prior to the 1929 crash.

Plans for another prestigious private club, the Seminole Golf Club, were initiated by some of the same people who had been instrumental in establishing the Bath and Tennis Club. Located north of Palm Beach, it was built for members from Hobe Sound and Palm Beach who wanted a real championship course. Chris Dunphy was a popular resident of Palm Beach before his death and was known in the area as "Mr. Golf." He described the Seminole course as one of the six best in the world.

One of the oldest clubs in town is the Sailfish Club, which was originally founded in 1910, and the club's burgee was first recorded in *Lloyd's Registry of Yachts* in 1914. The founders were interested in renewing the sport of angling for sailfish and other game fish. Originally the club rooms were at the Breakers Casino, and then moved to Whitehall before a permanent clubhouse was constructed in 1928 on the Lake Trail at the north end of the island. Backgammon, bingo, and one-armed bandits were the favorites in the friendly informal club. One of the early members remembers, "No one wore satins, minks, or brocades. They were for the Everglades Club. What we all loved about the Sailfish Club was its informality."

One of the most popular clubs in the twenties, the Club de Montmartre, no longer exists; however, the Mizner-designed building now houses the Society of the Four Arts. While it flourished in the mid-twenties, the Montmartre was an exclusive supper club with late-night dancing. In 1929 its name was changed to the Embassy Club.

Boxing was a popular sport in the twenties, and the Oasis Club, which was located behind the present main post office, was the scene of many bouts. The Oasis was an athletic club for men only, and ladies were originally allowed only on Friday night for the famous beefsteak suppers. In 1928 members relented and ladies were allowed from 4:30 P.M. until closing time.

Undoubtedly one of the most popular spots in town for lunch and dinner was the Patio, a famous restaurant that operated like a

Boxing at the Oasis Club.

Patio of Embassy Club built by Colonel Bradley.

club. The former maître d'hotel kept special tables reserved for the regulars such as the Pulitzers, Vanderbilts, and McLeans. The finest chefs from New York were brought down for the season to prepare the renowned lunches and dinners. Hot dishes were cooked in heavy black pots and brought to the table in the same pot. One of the most famous dishes was Seafood LaMaze, a cold dish of all kinds of seafood with Russian dressing served in handsome Mizner-blue crocks.

The Patio, which was located on Sunset Avenue and County Road, was a popular stopping-off place late in the evening for dancing and a snack. Meyer Davis and his orchestra played for many seasons, and one of the unique features of the building was a roof that rolled back exposing the gorgeous tropical skies. At some point in the evening the members of the orchestra (except the piano player) would disappear and then reappear on the roof, serenading the patrons with the popular hit of the day, "Florida, the Moon and You." The orchestra was often joined by headliners

51

such as Joe E. Lewis or Sophie Tucker, who would come to the Patio after appearing in Miami.

Another orchestra that was popular at the Patio in the 1930s was Val Ernie's. One of the frequent patrons, Kenneth Smith, the chairman of Pepsodent liked it so much that he bought a Lincoln for Val Ernie and gave the other four men in the band Pontiacs. Later, before the Patio closed, Smith bought a share of the business for the orchestra leader.

The private establishment in town that continued to maintain its excellent reputation over the years was Colonel Bradley's Beach Club. In 1923 Bradley had added chemin de fer to roulette and hazard, the only two games previously played in the club. The "chemmy" tables were extremely popular and it is estimated that over $3,000,000 changed hands that year from chemin de fer alone.

Colonel Edward R. Bradley and his niece, Peggy Bailey, on her wedding day.

Bradley raised his limits, which were now higher than Monte Carlo's, and the octagonal gambling room, decorated in Bradley's racing colors of green and white, was the scene of constant excitement—ladies and gentlemen in evening clothes would often wager $50,000 on the turn of a card.

The Beach Club's cuisine and buffet froid were famous all over the country. *Palm Beach Life* in February, 1928, described the opening-day buffet froid prepared by chef Jean Broca: "Among the fanciful creations . . . were an elaborately decorated boat containing a fish, a delectable house of sugar, an enormous crawfish in jelly, a huge baked ham ornamented with a ballet girl in bouffant skirts, a block of ice carved in the shape of an urn holding caviar and many other exotic and delicious hors d'oeuvres."

The Colony Club near the Beach Club also offered excellent food and entertainment. Many Palm Beachers entertained parties of twenty to thirty guests at the Gala Nights at the Colony. According to a former manager, one of the frequent patrons of the Colony was Philadelphian Arthur Strasburger, a wealthy widower. Many nights he escorted beautiful young ladies to the Colony, and before the night was over had given away a dazzling sum in tips . . . $20 for the hatcheck girl, $200 to the singer, $300 for the orchestra leader . . . and his dinner had only cost $20.

The Everglades Club continued to occupy a preeminent place in the social activities of the resort. Golfing activities were increased when the original nine-hole course was expanded to eighteen holes when parts of the lakefront were filled in in 1928. One of the most anticipated events of the winter season was the annual Bal Masque. The balls were famous for their fantastic decorations and the extravagant costumes worn by members for the occasion. It is reported that E. T. Stotesbury, who was a frequent first-prize winner, collected over 150 fancy-dress costumes with the Everglades Bal Masque in mind.

The end of the season was climaxed by the annual Coconuts Party when a group of prominent bachelors in town banded together to repay their hosts and hostesses for the invitations of the season. The first Coconuts Party was given at the Palm Beach Country Club in 1925, and the hosts included James Hyde, Caleb Bragg, Jack Rutherford, Lytle Hull, Rod Wanamaker, and Herbert Pulitzer. The Coconuts Party is still given today, but it now takes place at the Poinciana Club on New Year's Eve, and many of the members are sons of the original members.

Not all entertainments were completely social. At the grand estates groups of guests gathered to be entertained by the finest artists in the country. At Playa Reinte audiences of approximately 150 heard performances by Fritz Kreisler, and Metropolitan opera stars Elizabeth Rethberg and Benjamino Gigli. These private "at home" appearances were especially popular in the early twenties before there was a proper public showcase for the performing arts.

There was only one film theater operating in Palm Beach during the boom years of the early twenties. The Beaux Arts Theater, located on the roof of the Beaux Arts Fashion Center north of Bradley's, was a popular spot for watching the heroes of the silent screen. It was a truly unique place, for on a balmy night the sides of the theater could be opened so that patrons could look out over the lake. Mrs. John Emerson (Anita Loos) entertained friends there in 1926 with a private showing of *Gentlemen Prefer Blondes*, the film version of her book. In 1928 the Beaux Arts was renovated to show the new "see-and-hear" pictures.

Palm Beach's need for a more elaborate theater was answered when the Paramount Theater on the corner of Sunrise Avenue and North County Road opened in 1926. It was designed for silent films accompanied by music and for small live performances. The Mediterranean-style building featured an orchestra pit large enough to accommodate a full orchestra. It had nearly perfect acoustics.

The Paramount's architect, Joseph Urban, was an Austrian designer who had just completed alterations on the palace of the Queen of Egypt, was working on set decorations for Florenz Ziegfeld, and later would be the architect for the Metropolitan Opera House in New York. Local legend says that Urban made the preliminary drawing for the fan-shaped theater on a tablecloth in a New York restaurant. The building, which was financed by a syndicate of Boston and New York financiers, was unusual in that it incorporated shops and apartments with a moving picture theater and a typical Florida patio. The inside of the theater was decorated with murals depicting sea life, green silk appliqued walls painted with sea creatures, and a green cypress ceiling with rippled beams simulating the effect of being under water.

The most sought after seats in the Paramount were the boxes in the Diamond Horseshoe. These thirteen balcony boxes with gilded armchairs sold for $1,000 a box for the season. There were two openings a week on Sunday and Wednesday during the season,

Paramount Theater.

Interior of the Paramount Theater.

and black tie was traditional. It was necessary to make advance reservations for the two shows per day, and the nonbox tickets sold for $1 and $2.

The gala opening was held on January 9, 1927, with the premier of the film *Beau Geste* starring Ronald Colman. There was a full orchestra, with Alexander Basse conducting and Velazo at the Wurlitzer organ. The Miami *Herald* reported that the audience was made up of "the famous, the admired and the glamorous." In the center box were Mr. and Mrs. E. F. Hutton, Anthony Drexel Biddle, Jr., and Charles Munn. The audience also included Joseph Urban, Irving Berlin, Mr. and Mrs. E. T. Stotesbury and syndicate members, J. Leonard Repogle, and Arthur Keleher. Champagne was served after the opening, and ushers in white gloves escorted the ladies to their cars after the performance. (The ushers were still wearing white gloves in the forties.) Many movies had their first runs at the Paramount: *It* starring Clara Bow, *Faust* with Emil Jannings, *Casey at the Bat* with Wallace Beery, *Ben Hur* with Ramon Navarro and Francis X. Bushman, and *Love* with Greta Garbo and John Gilbert.

Live entertainment and shows were also featured, and the list of entertainers includes George Jessel, Eddie Cantor, Charlie Chaplin, Bob Hope, Mary Pickford, and Oscar Hammerstein. Shows to benefit charity were inaugurated and featured stars such as Will Rogers, who entertained for the Salvation Army in March, 1928.

One of the highlights of the Paramount's season became the annual Benefit for the Under-Privileged Children's Fund of the Kiwanis Club. The Kiwanians had originally made voluntary • contributions to support their health-care projects for the economically deprived children of Palm Beach County, but expenses soon rose to the point at which additional revenue was needed. Mrs. Arthur Hammerstein, the former Dorothy Dalton of the silent screen, became interested in the work of the Kiwanis Club, and in 1927 she assisted in producing the first show to benefit the fund. This is one of the oldest service club projects in the nation. The Orange Blossom Revue ran for forty years and featured stars such as Al Jolson, Eddie Cantor, Sophie Tucker, W. C. Fields, Victor Borge, and Danny Kaye. In 1929 the benefit featured a three-round boxing bout between Jack Dempsey and Babe Ruth. Another show in 1935 headlined George Gershwin playing his own compositions. The $400,000 raised during the show's existence is credited with helping over 170,000 children in Palm Beach County.

Florenz Ziegfeld and his wife, Billie Burke, were popular members of the resort community, and in 1926 Ziegfeld brought to Palm Beach one of the most spectacular productions ever to be staged in the area. *Palm Beach Nights,* which ran for two months and ten days, was the only Ziegfeld Follies not to originate on Broadway. Excitement was rampant prior to opening night, and bachelors of the day remember signs appearing all over town saying: FIFTY GIRLS ARE COMING!!!

The cast was headed by Morton Downey and Clare Luce; the score was by Rudolph Friml and Gene Buck; the lyrics were by Irving Caesar. Production credits went to Paris Singer, Tony Biddle, and Flo Ziegfeld. The show's hit song, "Florida, the Moon and You," became Palm Beach's theme song for many years.

One of the most extravagant Palm Beach estates built in the 1920s was Mar-a-Lago, the palatial home of Marjorie Merriweather Post, then Mrs. Edward F. Hutton. Designed by Marion Sims Wyeth (exterior plans) and Joseph Urban (interior design), the 122-room edifice took four years to build and was opened in 1927. The fairy-tale mansion, which still stands guard on the south end of

Entrance to Mar-a-Lago.

A view taken from the air of Mrs. Marjorie Merriweather Post's estate Mar-a-Lago. In the foreground is a nine-hole golf course; in the background, the Atlantic Ocean.
Mort Kaye Studios

Palm Beach across from the Bath and Tennis Club, sprawls across seventeen acres of manicured lawns and gardens. From the Great Window off the main dining room the Atlantic Ocean can be seen lapping at Mar-a-Lago's private beach, which is across South Ocean Boulevard and can be reached by a private tunnel under the road. To the west a private par-three golf course stretches to the shore of Lake Worth.

Marjorie Merriweather Post, reputed to have been one of the wealthiest women in the world with her holdings in the cereal company and General Foods, was an energetic, well-loved person who ran her life with order and precision even when she was in her eighties. Easily identifiable by her regal carriage, Mrs. Post was often referred to in newspaper and magazine articles as "The Queen of Palm Beach." Until her death in 1973, Mrs. Post maintained a home in Washington, D.C., at Hillwood, which now belongs to the Smithsonian Institution, and a summer camp in the Adirondacks in addition to her winter home in Palm Beach.

The opulent Mar-a-Lago seems to have been transplanted to this choice piece of coastline from another era. The mansion is built in the Hispano-Moresque style and combines decorative elements from the Spanish, Venetian, and Portuguese. A gold leaf ceiling in the living room is a copy of the Thousand-Wing Ceiling in the Accademia at Venice. Thirty-six thousand priceless antique Spanish tiles are set in the interior and exterior walls. The hundreds of sculptures and reliefs took Austria's Franz Barwig and his son three years of constant work to complete. The crescent-shaped house is flanked with graceful cloisters and topped with a seventy-foot tower which commands a spectacular view. The unique twelve-foot-long marble dining room table, made to order in the Medici Marble Works in Florence, is inlaid with semi-precious stones.

After Mar-a-Lago was completed, the Huttons entertained frequently in their showplace. One of the largest parties given the year after the mansion was finished was a dinner preceding the Everglades Bal Masque.

Even in the 1920s Mrs. Hutton opened her home for the benefit of the Animal Rescue League, and she continued this practice until her death. The Red Cross was another of her favorite charities. The Huttons also loved the theater and often brought down entire Broadway casts to entertain 200 with a full-length play. In 1930 they gave a performance of *Stepping Out*, and then treated the cast to a week's vacation at Mar-a-Lago. Another time the complete Ringling Brothers circus performed there.

In 1931 the Huttons bought the *Sea Cloud*, the largest private sailing vessel ever built, for $900,000. The four-masted square-rigged ship was 316 feet long and had two diesel engines plus nearly an acre of sail. She carried a crew of seventy-two, and the monthly payroll for the ship's crew was over $20,000. During World War II Mrs. Post loaned the *Sea Cloud* to the U. S. Government for one dollar a year. When Mrs. Post's third husband, Joseph Davies, served as American ambassador to Russia, they took the *Sea Cloud* with them and the Russians refused to believe it was privately owned.

After World War II, Mrs. Post's favorite way of entertaining was square dancing. It seems incongruous that the opulent Mar-a-Lago would be the setting for square dancing, but on Thursday and Sunday evenings the stately dance pavilion would echo with the

Sea Cloud—the Davies' yacht. Marjorie Merriweather Post was at one time married to Ambassador Joseph E. Davies.

Mr. and Mrs. Cliff Robertson (Dina Merrill) and Mrs. Marjorie Merriweather Post.
Mort Kaye Studios

commands of the caller as Mrs. Post's guests would "Promenade on" and "Swing their partners" in a good old-fashioned hoedown. One of Mrs. Post's daughters, the well-known actress Dina Merrill Robertson, remembers how her mother enjoyed the square dances. "She loved the exercise of square dancing, and that's why she particularly liked entertaining this way as she got older and did not play golf or other sports anymore."

Organization and punctuality were very important ingredients of the squre dances. The number of guests varied from thirty to as many as eighty. They were invited for cocktails at 7:30 P.M., and dinner, which was announced promptly at 8 P.M., was scheduled to last one hour. To allocate just one hour for serving dinner to eighty people would make many hostesses lose sleep the night before, but at Mar-a-Lago the kitchen always ran smoothly.

Ladies were escorted into the dining room by their dinner partners and all would be seated at round tables for eight or ten. The first course would already be on the table, and then the guests would select their main course from a buffet spread on the marble-inlaid dining room table. Dessert was passed to the individual tables.

At 9 P.M. musicians in cowboy hats and boots would parade into the dining room, playing gaily as they wove their way between the tables. This was the signal for the guests to follow the band and Mrs. Post into the pavilion. Professional dancers mingled with the guests and helped guide them through the intricacies of the square dance steps, but according to a frequent guest, Judge James R. Knott, "No one really cared how good a dancer you were." Usually at some point during the evening, Mrs. Post would dance a tango with a favorite partner while her guests watched. As one female guest remembers, "Mrs. Post was such a good dancer. She had such innate rhythm and timing that she could easily have been a professional dancer."

Sandwiches, cake, coffee, and drinks were served at 10:45 after the evening's dancing, and at 11 all would join hands and, with the caller leading them, sing a favorite goodnight song.

Mar-a-Lago was often filled with famous houseguests. One, the Queen of Norway, remarked of her hostess, "She lives like a queen!" Several years later two former employees of Buckingham Palace were working at Mar-a-Lago, and they asserted, "Mrs. Post lives better than a queen!"

Since Mrs. Marjorie Merriweather Post's death, Mar-a-Lago has remained closed. Her will bequeathed Mar-a-Lago to the United States government as a place to entertain foreign heads of state visiting this country. But even with a trust fund to maintain the palatial mansion and grounds, it is not certain that the estate can be reopened. Mar-a-Lago belongs to another era, to the fabulous twenties in Palm Beach.

In their heyday the durability of Mar-a-Lago and the rest of the buildings in Palm Beach was tested by a ferocious enemy. On the Sunday evening of September 16, 1928, a great killer hurricane hit Palm Beach County.

The thrust of the hurricane was in the Lake Okeechobee area, and this is where the great loss of life occurred. Fortunately most of the houses in Palm Beach were boarded up and battened down, closed for the off-season. Almost all the winter visitors were still in the North, and the lake was relatively bare of yachts. Consequently there was no loss of life in Palm Beach, but 1,500 homes and 500 business houses were damaged. The total damage in the town alone was estimated at $10,000,000.

Many of the homes in the north end around the inlet were under seven feet of water, and the pier at the Breakers was completely destroyed. The hotel itself lost part of the roof and much of its

Hurricane of 1928.

landscaping. One of the hardest hit buildings in town was the gracious old Royal Poinciana Hotel. Part of the middle section of the hotel was lost.

The painters, contractors, and landscape men working at the estates along South Ocean Boulevard were busy preparing for the opening of another glamorous season when the stock market crashed on Black Thursday, October 24, 1929.

For some the financial debacle, the results of which would sweep the world, would make little change in their life-style. A well-known present-day historian remarked that it was "the difference between the rich and the super rich." For the elite who suffered minimal losses, life in Palm Beach went on as before. They swam and lunched at the Bath and Tennis, played golf at Seminole, Gulf Stream, or the Everglades, partied at their clubs, and gambled at Bradley's. Diamond Horseshoe boxes at the Paramount sold for the same price as before. However, even these people seemed to use charge accounts more than previously, according to the former manager of one of the popular clubs.

For others who owned beautiful homes in Palm Beach, the Depression meant the end of their winter sojourns. Many houses stayed boarded up and soon the peeling paint and unkempt lawns bore testimony to the effects of the crash. Some who had made a habit of wintering at the fashionable hotels stayed away. The hotel business was badly affected. The Royal Poinciana closed its doors in 1933 and was finally demolished in 1935.

Southern Florida suffered threefold during the early thirties. The area's economy was still staggering under the bursting of the Florida real estate bubble when the Depression followed on the heels of the 1928 hurricane. In 1933, the worst year of the Depression, the national unemployment rate was at a staggering 25 percent, but South Florida unemployment was double that figure. People queued in bread lines in West Palm Beach. When it was rumored that there was going to be a run on the banks in West Palm Beach, Colonel Edward Bradley lent over $500,000 to keep them open. Edward Hutton, Lou Kaufman, and E. T. Stotesbury also lent funds. The Huttons gave a thousand food boxes to area families in 1932.

Even the Everglades Club, that symbol of social impeccability, almost went under during the Depression years. In 1928 Paris Singer, in need of ready cash, arranged for a bond issue secured by a mortgage on the club and its properties.

The sprawling Royal Poinciana Hotel, 1903–1930.

By 1933 the club was in receivership. In 1936 twenty-one of the club members formed a Protective Syndicate to purchase the club property from the trustees for the bondholders. The members' subscriptions ranged from $2,000 to $100,000, and totaled $535,000. It is difficult today to believe that such a sum would have been sufficient to purchase this outstanding property, but the action of the Protective Syndicate saved the Everglades Club.

Life in the thirties in Palm Beach continued in the grand style. The pace was a little slower than during the Roaring Twenties, but as the national economy picked up in the last half of the decade, hotels were again crowded with those who followed the tropical sun. The elite of Palm Beach and Miami society frequented the Phipps Field at Gulf Stream to watch the Phippses, Winston and

Raymond Guest, Laddie Sanford, and the Firestones from Miami compete in triweekly polo matches.

The Duke and Duchess of Windsor arrived in Palm Beach soon after the Duke's abdication in 1936. They occupied an apartment at the Everglades Club, and flocks of visitors crowded the street below eager to glimpse the royal pair. Sometimes the Windsors would appear on their balcony, greeted by applause and cheers, to wave to the crowd. The Windsors continued to make an annual pilgrimage to Palm Beach until the Duke's death, and their arrival would signal the start of "the little season."

President Hoover visited Palm Beach on New Year's Eve in 1932. The next year would bring Roosevelt's New Deal to the rest of the country, but in Palm Beach the society magazines neglected to mention the economic turmoil. For those who were there, the Everglades Masquerade Balls, the Kiwanis benefit, and founding of the Round Table and the Four Arts Society filled their busy days and nights. Jimmy Cromwell, Mrs. Stotesbury's son, who entertained at his home, Malmaison, on the grounds of his mother's estate, gave parties that were as talked about as his stepfather's birthday parties had been. Palm Beach was having a good, good time.

World War II and the succeeding era brought many changes. Because of the ideal climate, wartime training sites and operations were set up in the area. The Coast Guard commandeered the Biltmore Hotel for a training school, and the Breakers served briefly as a convalescent center. Local residents were reminded that the country was at war each time they looked at the beach and saw patrolling U. S. warships silhouetted on the horizon. Rumors of German U-boats in the area took on new substance as Allied boats were sunk off the Florida coast. One hundred eleven American ships were lost to U-boat attacks off the coast of Florida during World War II, and five of these occurred in the vicinity of Palm Beach. Survivors were treated at local hospitals.

Palm Beach celebrated the Allied victory with the rest of the nation, then quickly changed her wartime demeanor back to that of a happy vacationland. The visitors still came, but they stayed longer, and there were more permanent residents. Those who vacationed here had followed the advice of signs that appeared in the thirties, urging "stay until May." Then, with air conditioning, they found they were happy to live here all year long.

Palm Beach is still a playgound for the rich; the hotel life is still

Nighttime view of the Biltmore Hotel.

glamorous, but there is a more permanent character to its population, increasingly the well-traveled and well-educated, including many professional people, choose it above all other locations as a place to live, work, and relax in beautiful tropical surroundings.

The Town of Palm Beach has worked hard to retain its uniqueness; it has legislated to provide beauty and comfort for its residents and visitors. There is excellent police protection, and trash and garbage are collected six days a week. Strict zoning laws prohibit the rise of another concrete jungle similar to the one that has engulfed the coastline to the south. For the enjoyment of the visitors, construction is regulated during the winter season. Building cannot start until 9 A.M. between December 1 and May 1, and all heavy work such as blasting and bulldozing is prohibited during this same period. Aircraft are forbidden to make landings in the town, and one of the few exceptions ever granted was for President Kennedy to land his helicopter here when the Kennedy house functioned as the winter White House. Palm Beach has no mortuaries, cemeteries, or hospitals, although almost every other conceivable service is available in the town.

Palm Beach is no longer the sleepy little resort settlement that it was in Flagler's day, but a quiet community of 10,000 living in single-family homes and condominiums behind beautifully manicured lawns and tropical hedges. Residents pride themselves that Palm Beach is a very civilized place to live. It is a place with a distinctive style of living, which shows particularly in the way Palm Beachers entertain. Since Palm Beach attracts discerning, well-traveled people from all over the world both as residents and visitors, the standards of entertaining are exceptionally high. From elaborate balls to more simple dinners at home, most hostesses seem to agree that the key ingredient of a successful party is interesting people, but they also pay great attention to the settings, arrangements, and food which their guests will enjoy. This entertaining is done with a distinctive flair, a Palm Beach style.

A view of Palm Beach taken from the air.

"The thing that has given me the greatest pleasure in making my grandfather's home, Whitehall, into a museum is giving people exposure to an elegant home, a place where people lived graciously."

—JEAN FLAGLER MATTHEWS

"Palm Beach is the least changed place of any place we have ever been. It has marvelous beauty and serenity—and it is a tremendous privilege to live here."

—ENID HAUPT

"Palm Beach should be treated like the south of France or Italy. It has a different ambiance than any place else in the United States."

—MRS. DOUGLAS FAIRBANKS, JR.

"Palm Beach is a permanent colony now. People are here for four seasons and there are many different kinds of entertaining. It is a many faceted thing."

—MRS. WALTER GUBELMANN

"People think that every night's a party in Palm Beach. That's just not true. I live the same kind of life as I would in any other place. It's just that this is a more beautiful place."

—MORTON DOWNEY

"A great many people escape to the peace, tranquillity, and beauty of Palm Beach. When I awake in the morning to blue sky and an azure ocean, I am able to forget so many of the problems that exist in the world today."

—NATHAN APPLEMAN

PART 2

Palm Beach Entertains

Mr. and Mrs. Norberto Azqueta's party for their children featured a Wizard of Oz theme. *Bob Davidoff Studios*

Behind the hedges in Palm Beach gala parties go on much as they did decades ago. It is a town that has a fine tradition of gracious entertaining, where hostesses plan their parties with considerable care and excellent food is presented.

Many guests coming to Palm Beach for the first time comment on the superior quality of the food served at the private parties and at the clubs. Most Palm Beach hosts and hostesses are knowledgeable and well-traveled gourmets who delight in a great variety of food. The private clubs excel in their cuisine because of the discriminating tastes of the members, who demand high standards of excellence. The chefs at the Bath and Tennis Club, the Beach Club, the Palm Beach Country Club, the Everglades Club, the Poinciana Club, and the Sailfish Club have earned their international reputations.

Much of the entertainment centers around charity affairs. Every type of ball, auction, cocktail party, brunch, and sporting tournament is sponsored to raise funds for worthwhile causes. In the Town of Palm Beach in 1975, $6,895,339 was raised for charity.

Some private parties are as varied as the life-styles of the Palm Beachers who give them. Jean Flagler Matthews, the granddaughter of Henry Morrison Flagler, remembers the dazzling tables set by her mother, Mrs. Harry Harkness Flagler, for her frequent dinner parties. Today elegance and tradition are integral parts of her life. When she entertains at high tea or midday Sunday dinner, she uses the exquisite linens and laces and the fine china and silver that were her mother's. Even without guests, she enjoys her table set with the lovely heirloom belongings. In selecting her Palm Beach home, Mrs. Matthews looked for one with a dining room that lent itself to formality because she believes everything, especially fine food, should be in a proper and appropriate setting.

Their present-day preference of Mr. and Mrs. A. Atwater Kent, Jr., for small, formal dinner parties follows a tradition set by Mr. Kent's mother. When wintering in Palm Beach in the twenties, Mrs. Kent preferred entertaining guests at tables of six, since that number allowed for several congenial conversations or permitted one person to "hold forth" easily. Low centerpieces made it comfortable to see and talk across the table. Guests were expected to arrive promptly and depart at a reasonable hour. Many Palm Beachers still honor an eleven o'clock departure hour, as they may be out or entertaining almost every evening during the season.

"Parties that are crammed in with great piles of people" are the current choice of Mrs. George Schrafft, a vivacious hostess who loves to entertain informally. Since her husband likes simple American food, and because she "hates the caterers' campaign," Judy Schrafft does most of the cooking herself. For a buffet for sixty people on the anniversary of Paul Revere's ride, she spent the previous day using scissors to cut round steak for her chili and cleaning 400 stalks of asparagus.

Many hostesses like to entertain a large crowd at home with a dinner dance. Society orchestra leader Marshall Grant plays about 400 engagements a year, most of them in Palm Beach and many of them held in lawn tents for groups of 150. Marshall Grant feels that the secret of a truly great party is "a hostess who gets into her party. If you have a nervous hostess, you don't have a chance." He has these suggestions for planning a dinner dance: provide plenty of places by the dance floor to put drinks, don't seat older nondancers next to the band, and don't have too large a dance floor; it will spoil a party. "Figure half the couples will be on the dance floor at one time and then allow seven square feet per couple," he advises. He has noticed that people dance counterclockwise, and feels the piano should be placed so that the pianist can see the people dancing toward him.

Not all the grand Palm Beach parties are staged at night. Cuban-born Mr. and Mrs. Norberto Azqueta give an afternoon costume party for their children's friends each spring. Mrs. Azqueta created the party to take the place of carnival season, which the family had enjoyed when they lived in Cuba. For these parties the grounds of the family compound have been transformed into such faraway places as Disneyland, Mexico, the

Orient, or Wonderland. A ferris wheel, a superslide, cotton candy machines, an organ grinder with his monkey—all have been brought in for the children.

Lian Azqueta keeps a careful record of each party—her invitation list, seating arrangement, photographs of decorations and favors, the menu, notes on ordering and prices, and all the details to make preparation for the next one easier.

Palm Beach party ideas are as varied as the tastes of the hosts and hostesses who give them, and every conceivable type of entertaining crowds the season. What makes a Palm Beach party? Imaginative planning, excellent food, and careful attention to detail are what make the difference. The ideas and recipes that follow are designed for the hostess who wants to adopt for herself the Palm Beach style.

The home of Mr. and Mrs. Stephen Sanford. *Mort Kaye Studios*

The guest house (left) and residence of Mr. and Mrs. James Akston. *Bruce Hubbard*

The Akstons' sculpture garden. *Mort Kaye Studios*

Hors D'Oeuvres and Appetizers

Legend has it that the ancient Greeks were the first to savor the tasty delights of an hors d'oeuvre trolley, and today's Palm Beachers are still enjoying cocktail food designed to stimulate the appetite. Whether the appetizers precede an elaborate or a simple dinner or are served at a large cocktail party, they are the favorites of many hostesses.

Lesly Smith, whose husband, Earl E. T. Smith, is the former ambassador to Cuba and the mayor of Palm Beach, frequently gives big cocktail parties around the holidays or winter golf tournaments when their many friends are in town—"Sometimes when you have a houseguest that everyone is dying to meet, it's the only way to entertain." One notable invitation from the Smiths was to a reception for 100 guests in honor of Senator George Murphy when he was guest lecturer at the Society of the Four Arts. Mrs. Smith serves a variety of appetizers so that there is something to please everyone; and if a buffet dinner follows cocktails, she always offers a choice of two entrees.

Mrs. Stephen Sanford entertains in a myriad of ways, but she also prefers a large cocktail party when she wants to introduce a visitor. A Spanish portrait painter was the recent honored guest at cocktails for over 200 people in her oceanfront Mizner home, Los Incas. The large rooms open into one another, relieving the usual cocktail party crush by the front door. Mrs. Sanford invites guests from 6 to 8 P.M. and provides many good finger foods and beverages but no music. "Music stops all good conversation at a cocktail party," Mrs. Sanford says. Trays of hot and cold canapes are always passed rather than served from a buffet table. A favorite hors d'oeuvre, flown down from New York, is smoked salmon, cut paper-thin and seasoned with oil, capers, and lemon and served on toast rounds. One specialty of the Sanford's Cuban chef, Manolo, is small bite-sized hamburgers broiled with a tiny island of catsup and mustard sauce in the middle.

"Big bowls of food—especially seafood" are the choice of Mrs. Samuel Rautbord, whose lakeside home is filled with modern art treasures. For her cocktail food she will serve platters of crab legs and bowls of shrimp accompanied by several different sauces.* A luxury item that she sometimes indulges in is stone crabs that have been shelled so that only a small piece of the outside shell remains for a handle to use in dipping it in a mustard sauce. When the committee on the Archives of American Art of the Smithsonian visited the Rautbord's Palm Beach home as part of a bicentennial art tour of America, Dorothy Rautbord served one of her favorite hors d'oeuvres—new potatoes boiled or baked in the skins, opened slightly and topped with sour cream and caviar. She prefers to have hot hors d'oeuvres passed to the guests, but cold trays are placed strategically around the room, including the dining room. Mrs. Rautbord often uses a beautiful Japanese silk obi sash as a runner on her dining room table on such occasions.

Mrs. Rautbord's neighbors, Mr. and Mrs. James Akston, also have a magnificent lakeside home filled with modern art. The Akstons' La Ronda is one of the new showplaces in Palm Beach. Their favorite place for cocktails is in a lovely sculpture terrace that features several large pieces set around a fountain in a small pool paved with malachite. A large sculpture carved in onyx and de-signed by Mr. Akston, who is an artist as well as an art collector, dominates the pool. To protect their guests from the tropical sun there are two large Swiss umbrellas made of natural linen, which make a startling contrast to the stark modernity of the sculptures and the lush tropical foliage.

Most Palm Beach hosts and hostesses seem to agree that they allow only thirty to forty-five minutes for cocktails preceding dinner—especially since most of them serve wine with the meal. One well-known hostess who prefers a long, relaxed cocktail time combined with cards is Mrs. George W. Blabon. Lilly Blabon loves to invite a group of twelve for cards at 5 P.M. followed by dinner at 8. During the card game, she likes to serve appetizers such as shrimp; crab fingers; pâte; water chestnuts soaked in wine, wrapped in bacon, and then broiled; and Bermuda puffs (small

*Recipes on page 77 and following.

rounds of toast topped with a slice of onion and mayonnaise, sprinkled with Romano cheese, and broiled until puffed and brown). After dinner, the guests again return to their cards.

How much liquor, ice, and help is needed for a cocktail party for 100 people? This is a question often asked of Palm Beach restaurateur Phil Romano, and this is the formula he has devised to aid in party planning: When preparing for 100 people for cocktails, plan two drinks per person, allowing twenty drinks per quart bottle of liquor. There should be one waitress for every twenty people, and one bartender for every 100. Order one pound of cubed ice per person and one seven-ounce bottle of mix per person. Mr. Romano feels that in Palm Beach scotch is still the favorite liquor, but vodka and white wine are steadily gaining in popularity.

Many of the recipes that follow in this section can be used both as cocktail food for large or small groups and as a first course to be served at the table.

The following three sauces are excellent served with cold seafood.

Mustard Sauce

2 tablespoons Dijon-style mustard
3 tablespoons boiling water
½ cup olive oil
¼ teaspoon salt
freshly ground black pepper
1 teaspoon lemon juice
1 tablespoon finely chopped parsley

Place the mustard in a small mixing bowl. Stir in the boiling water. Add the olive oil, drop by drop, beating constantly with a wire whisk, until the oil is completely absorbed. Add the salt, pepper, lemon juice, and parsley. Adjust the seasoning.

Makes 1¼ cup of sauce.

May also be used as a dipping sauce for cold artichokes.

Russian Dressing with Caviar

1 cup mayonnaise
½ cup catsup
½ cup chili sauce
½ cup chopped pimento
2 tablespoons chopped chives
1 tablespoon chopped parsley
1 hard-boiled egg, chopped
1 tablespoon lemon juice
2 tablespoons Beluga caviar
dash of cayenne and paprika

Mix all of the above ingredients, chill, and serve with large bowls of chilled boiled shrimp.
Makes approximately 3 cups of sauce.

This is a favorite dipping sauce of Mrs. Samuel Rautbord.

Scandia Sauce

1 tablespoon prepared mustard
1 teaspoon sugar
1½ tablespoons wine vinegar
½ teaspoon salt
dash white pepper
4 tablespoons salad oil
1 teaspoon lemon juice
1 tablespoon finely chopped fresh dill

Combine the ingredients and allow to stand several hours before serving.
Serves 6.

Shrimp Remoulade

4 tablespoons horseradish mustard
½ cup tarragon vinegar
2 tablespoons catsup
1 tablespoon paprika

½ teaspoon cayenne pepper
1 teaspoon salt
1 whole garlic clove
1 cup salad oil
½ cup finely minced green onions with tops
½ cup finely minced celery
2 hard-boiled eggs, finely chopped
2 pounds of small shrimp, boiled and cleaned

In a large bowl, mix the mustard, vinegar, catsup, paprika, pepper, and salt. Put garlic through a garlic press and add to mixture. Next add the oil, beating thoroughly. Add the onions, celery, and eggs. Pour this mixture over the shrimp and chill in the refrigerator for at least 4 to 5 hours.
Serves 8 to 10.

This may be made a day in advance. If passed with cocktails, strain the shrimp before serving. If used as a first course, serve on a bed of lettuce.

Scampi Hollandaise

2 pounds jumbo or large shrimp, cleaned
4 tablespoons lemon juice
4 tablespoons olive oil
½ cup white wine or vermouth
1 teaspoon salt
½ teaspoon pepper
1½ cups warm Hollandaise Sauce (recipe page 106)

Preheat oven to broil. Place shrimp in a large bowl. Sprinkle with the lemon juice, olive oil, wine, salt, and pepper. Stir to combine. Marinate, covered, in the refrigerator 2 to 3 hours. Remove marinated shrimp with a slotted spoon and arrange in a shallow baking dish in one layer. Broil on rack nearest heating element for 3 to 4 minutes. Turn and broil another 3 to 4 minutes. Spoon the warm Hollandaise over the cooked shrimp. Set under broiler just until top is brown, about 2 minutes.
Serves 6 to 8.

Mushroom Strudel

1 package (l pound) refrigerated phyllo pastry (can be purchased in
   specialty stores)
3½ sticks of sweet butter (14 ounces)
2 pounds mushrooms, finely chopped
2 cloves garlic, minced
¼ cup of sherry
½ teaspoon salt
⅛ teaspoon pepper
4 tablespoons chopped parsley
4 tablespoons chives, chopped
1 cup sour cream
½ cup bread crumbs

Preheat oven to 375°. Sauté in a large frying pan the mushrooms
and garlic in 1½ sticks of butter over moderately high heat for 8 to
10 minutes. Add sherry and cook until it is evaporated. Add salt,
pepper, parsley, and chives. Remove from heat and fold in the
sour cream. Set aside.

Melt remaining 1½ sticks of butter in a saucepan. Open 2 sheets
of phyllo pastry. Brush 1 tablespoon of the melted butter on the
first sheet to edges. Sprinkle with 1 tablespoon bread crumbs. Put
second sheet on the first and repeat with butter and bread crumbs.
Using a slotted spoon, so most of the excess liquid drains off,
spread ¼ mushroom mixture over the sheet, leaving a 2-inch
margin at top and bottom edges. Roll up (as for jelly roll), ending
with the seam on the bottom. Paint with butter, cover with a wet
towel until ready to cook. Prepare the remaining 3 rolls in the same
manner as directed above.

Place on a baking dish or cookie sheet and bake for 20 minutes.
Let cool. Freeze until firm and cut into slices while still frozen. Heat
at 350° for 15 minutes, standing slices on side like a pinwheel.

Yields: 4 logs (8 slices each)

*Important note: Keep a damp towel over the phyllo pastry before you
work with it and build the strudel on damp towels because the pastry dries
out quickly.*

Spinach Cheese Squares

4 tablespoons butter
3 eggs
1 cup flour
1 cup milk
1 teaspoon salt
1 teaspoon baking powder
1 pound Monterey Jack cheese or any other mild white cheese (grated)
2 packages chopped spinach, thawed

Preheat oven to 350°.

In a 9 x 13 x 2 baking pan melt the butter in the oven. Remove from oven. In a large mixing bowl, beat the eggs, then add the flour, milk, salt, and baking powder. Mix these ingredients well. Add the cheese and thawed spinach. Pour all ingredients into baking pan and bake for 35 minutes. Remove from oven, cool for 45 minutes in order to set. Cut into bite-sized squares.

To freeze: Place squares on a cookie sheet and allow to freeze, then transfer into plastic bags. Before serving, remove from bags, place on cookie sheet, heat in oven at 325° for 12 minutes.

Yield: 25 appetizers.

Mozzarella Stuffed Mushrooms

1 pound medium mushrooms (about 24)
¼ cup butter or margarine, melted
⅓ cup finely chopped mozzarella cheese
1 tablespoon seasoned bread crumbs
¼ cup sliced pimiento-stuffed olives

Preheat oven to broil.

Remove stems from mushrooms caps. Gently toss caps in melted butter in a small bowl. Place caps, cut side up, in a flat pan large enough to hold them in a single layer. Broil 3 to 5 minutes. In a small bowl combine the mozzarella cheese and bread crumbs. Spoon the cheese mixture into the mushroom caps and top each filled cap with an olive slice. When ready to serve, place under the broiler for 3 to 5 minutes to melt the cheese.

Makes 24 canapes.

This can be prepared earlier in the day up to the point of the final broiling. Refrigerate and finish broiling just before serving.

Chili Cheese

1 pound cheddar cheese, grated
1 large onion finely chopped
1 cup mayonnaise
1 teaspoon salt
1 teaspoon chili powder
60 toasted rounds

Preheat oven to broil.
Combine first 5 ingredients in a large mixing bowl. Spread on the toasted rounds and place on a large cookie sheet. Place under broiler until the cheese is melted.
refrigerator for several days.
Makes 60 canapes.

The filling stores well in the refrigerator for several days.

Toasted Rounds For Cocktail Canapes

15 slices of white bread
olive oil (enough to be 1 inch deep in frying pan)

Cut crusts off bread. Cut bread into 4 rounds. Fry in oil over medium-high heat until bread turns lightly brown. Fry both sides. Drain on toweling. These freeze well. Reheat before serving. Use in place of crackers when serving hors d'oeuvres.
Yields 60 rounds.

Cheese and Sausage Rolls

16 sausage links
16 slices white bread
1 cup shredded processed American cheese
¼ cup butter or margarine, softened

Preheat oven to 400°.

Cook and drain sausage links according to package directions. Trim crusts from bread; roll bread flat. Mix cheese and butter. Spread this mixture on each side of each slice of bread. Roll a sausage link in each slice of bread. Bake on greased baking sheet for 10 to 12 minutes. Slice into thirds and serve.

Makes 48 appetizers.

This can be made with cooked asparagus spears in place of sausage, and cheddar cheese substituted for American cheese.

Cheese Boxes

¾ pound sharp cheese
1½ pounds butter
2 egg whites
pinch of salt
1 loaf thin-sliced white bread (2 pounds)

Preheat oven to 375°.

Cut cheese into small cubes. In medium pan melt the butter and cheese over a low heat. Whip the egg whites with a pinch of salt until stiff. Add melted cheese mixture to egg whites a little at a time and mix well. Take 2 slices of bread at a time and cut off the crusts. Spread cheese mixture between slices very sparingly. Cut into 4 blocks or triangles or finger shapes. Coat sides and top very lightly with cheese mixture. Do not coat the bottom. Lay the sections on cookie sheets and bake for 12 to 15 minutes.

Yields 60 to 70 pieces.

To make ahead of time, do not bake. Place prepared pieces on cookie sheet and cool until the cheese sets. Refrigerate or freeze in a container with waxed paper between the layers. Remove from refrigerator or freezer and allow to reach room temperature before baking as directed. These will keep indefinitely in the freezer.

Baked Clams

4 tablespoons butter or oil
¼ cup chopped onion
2 tablespoons chopped parsley
2 cloves garlic, minced

½ teaspoon oregano
2 cups fresh bread crumbs
4 cans (8 ounces each) minced clams, drained almost dry
salt and freshly ground pepper
½ cup Parmesan cheese, grated
6 large or 12 small scallop shells

Preheat oven to 375°.

Melt butter in large skillet and sauté onion, parsley, and garlic for 2 minutes. Stir in oregano and bread crumbs and cook 2 minutes. Add minced clams and season with salt and pepper. Spoon into scallop shells and top with grated cheese. Bake 20 to 30 minutes until browned and bubbly.

These may be assembled in advance, refrigerated, and baked just before serving.

Soups

Soups seem to be a special Palm Beach favorite, particularly served cold. Several hostesses like to offer the soup course informally in the same room in which cocktails have been served. One hostess brings in her favorite tureen on a large tray and serves from it. Another suggests serving a cold soup (especially one that is an interesting color) in large, oversized crystal wineglasses.

Mrs. Douglas Fairbanks, Jr., is particularly fond of a hot soup served at the table as a first course. She enjoys using her collection of beautiful polished abalone shells, which are heated and filled with a creamy fish chowder.* The shells sparkle on brown china on a white linen cloth, reflecting the brown and white decor of her charming small dining room. She had been so pleased with the brown tortoiseshell vinyl wall-covering in the dining room of her first Palm Beach home that she has repeated the effect in her new home on the Lake Trail. Mary Lee Fairbanks never orders flowers from the florist and uses very little silver in her table decorations. She arranges dainty flowers in Waterford jelly cups for the center of the table, or she makes a centerpiece of fresh fruits and vegetables. She never issues black tie invitations because she feels that "people expect more when you say black tie." Her favorite dinner group is eight, but occasionally she will entertain sixteen to twenty-four, seating them at additional round tables. She serves the wine in the bottle without decanting it since she thinks "the wine should stay where it lives." Bottles of both red and white wine are placed on each table. The Fairbanks like to have interesting guests from the arts and the political world, and favor an evening of good conversation rather than games or music.

The former American ambassador to Pakistan, Benjamin Oehlert, loved the oyster stew at the Oyster Bar in New York's Grand Central Station so much that he went into his Palm Beach kitchen to see if he could duplicate it. After many tries he came up

*Recipe on page 90.

Former Ambassador and Mrs. Benjamin Oehlert have an apartment in the Everglades Club. *Mort Kaye Studios*

with a recipe* using twelve ingredients, and often entertains his visitors with this delicious dish.

Soups, hot or cold, light or hearty, embellish any meal. Many hostesses improvise a basic stock with what is left in the refrigerator. Mrs. F. Warrington Gillet's chef cleans the refrigerator every three days and uses all the bones and leftover vegetables to make stock for soup. He cooks it for several hours, strains it, and then stores it for later use.

Cold Madras Soup

1 can (10½ ounces) beef bouillon
1 can (10½ ounces) condensed green pea soup, undiluted
1 can (10½ ounces) tomato madrilene (red consommé)
2 cups light cream
1 tablespoon lemon juice
1 tablespoon curry powder
salt and pepper
1 or 2 tart apples, chopped

Combine the three soups and heat until well blended in a 2½-quart saucepan. Cool. Add the cream, lemon juice, curry powder, and salt and pepper. Chill. Serve very cold in bouillon cups, over the finely chopped apples.
Serves 6 to 8.

Because the ingredients travel well, Cold Madras Soup would be an interesting addition to a camping trip.

Striped Avocado Soup

3 cans (10½ ounces each) tomato madrilene
3 ripe avocados
3 tablespoons sour cream
3 tablespoons mayonnaise
1½ teaspoons minced onion
salt and pepper to taste
2½ tablespoons lemon juice

*Recipe on page 90.

Divide one can of the madrilene between 6 to 8 clear sherbet glasses, or small ramekins, to make one layer. Place in refrigerator to set. Mash avocado with remaining ingredients and spoon half of it, divided among the glasses, on top of the set madrilene. Divide another can of madrilene, carefully pouring it over the soft avocado mixture, using a teaspoon to "float" it on. Refrigerate this layer to set and then use the rest of the avocado mixture to make another layer. Gently pour over the third can of madrilene. Refrigerate until set. Garnish with some leftover avocado mixture or a dollop of sour cream.

Serves 6 to 8.

Mrs. Ellis Johnson uses this red and green layered soup for a perfect beginning of a December dinner.

Gazpacho

2 large cloves garlic
1 large onion, sliced
1 can (10 ounce) Mexican tomatoes with green chiles
2 green peppers, seeded and coarsely chopped
1 teaspoon salt
½ teaspoon pepper
½ cup vinegar
½ cup vegetable oil
1½ cups tomato juice
½ teaspoon cumin
8 eggs, beaten
Garnishes: chopped green pepper
           chopped celery
           toasted croutons

In a blender, place all of the ingredients except the eggs and blend until smooth. (It will require several separate blendings for entire recipe.) Add some of the eggs to each batch after it has been blended and blend again until they are used up.

Make the day before and chill in the refrigerator. Serve in chilled cups garnished with 1 heaping teaspoon of each of the garnishes.

Serves 6 to 8.

Crabmeat Soup

3 tablespoons butter
3 tablespoons flour
5 cups chicken broth
½ teaspoon curry powder
1 cup heavy cream
1 pound lump crabmeat
salt and white pepper to taste
croutons or parsley

Melt butter in large 2½-quart saucepan. Stir in flour and cook slowly for 3 minutes, stirring constantly. Add stock and blend well with wire whisk. Mix curry with a little of the stock and strain into soup. Cook slowly, uncovered for ½ hour. Add cream, crabmeat, salt and pepper. Serve hot with croutons or cold with parsley.
Serves 6 to 8.

Sea Cloud Chowder

1 red snapper (4 pounds)
1 quart cold water
1 teaspoon salt
½ cup salt pork, diced
¾ cup finely diced onion
½ cup diced green pepper
½ cup diced celery
4 cups raw cubed potatoes
1 quart light cream
¼ cup butter
¼ cup flour
chopped parsley to garnish

Place whole fish in cold water, add salt, and cook until fish flakes, about 15 minutes. Remove fish from pot. Flake and pick out the bones. Return fish head and bones to pot and simmer about 1 hour. Strain stock, and return stock to pot. Fry salt pork until golden brown; add onion and green pepper. Cook 10 minutes, then add to stock along with celery and potatoes. Cook vegetables until potatoes are tender, about 15 minutes. Add cream, heat, then add flaked fish. In a small saucepan melt ¼ cup butter, then stir ¼

cup flour into the butter. Add this mixture to the soup. Sprinkle with chopped parsley or dill before serving.
Serves 6 to 8.

This was a special favorite of the guests of Mrs. Marjorie Merriweather Post. The chowder was named after her 316 foot yacht Sea Cloud.

Fairbanks Chowder

1½ pounds haddock, or any firm white fish
1½ cups cold water
⅜ cup salt pork or 5 strips lean bacon, chopped
3 cups thinly sliced raw potatoes
⅓ cup cup chopped onion
1 cup water
3 cups milk
1½ cups light cream
1½ tablespoons butter
salt and paprika and pepper
¼ cup chopped parsley

In a saucepan, place the fish and cold water. Simmer, covered, for 10 minutes. Lift out fish and remove skin and bones. Flake and set aside. Reserve stock.

In another large saucepan, place the bacon and cook slowly for 10 minutes, stirring, being sure not to brown it. Drain off the grease. To the bacon add the potatoes, onions, ½ cup water, and the reserved stock. Simmer uncovered for 15 minutes. Stir for a minute to "break up" the potatoes. Fifteen to twenty minutes before serving, add the fish, milk, cream, salt, pepper, and paprika to taste. Heat slowly; do not boil. Garnish with the parsley
Serves 6 to 8.

This may be prepared ahead of time. Add the flaked fish before reheating.

Benjamin Oehlert's Oyster Stew

6 tablespoons butter
2 pints select oysters (frying size)
2 pints half and half
1 teaspoon salt

¼ teaspoon pepper
1 tablespoon Worcestershire sauce
1 teaspoon Accent
¼ teaspoon Tabasco
¼ teaspoon onion powder
½ teaspoon celery salt
¼ teaspoon garlic powder
pinch of cayenne

Place the butter in a large 2½-quart saucepan and add the oysters with their liquid. Cook over high heat and boil for 3 minutes. Remove from heat and add slightly warmed half and half and remaining ingredients. Heat very slowly until first bubbles appear. Do not boil. Correct seasoning. Serve with paprika or hickory salt if desired.

Serves 6 to 8.

Pozole

1 large fresh pork hock, split
1 stewing chicken
2 quarts water
1 can (16 ounces) whole tomatoes
2 cans (16 ounces each) hominy, drained
2 medium-sized onions, finely chopped
4 teaspoons salt

Fresh vegetable relishes:

shredded lettuce
chopped radishes
sliced green onions
chopped avocado
sliced mushrooms
shredded Monterey Jack cheese
2 limes, cut into wedges

Place the pork hock and chicken into a large kettle with the water, tomatoes, hominy, onions, and salt. Simmer 2 to 3 hours, covered, or until the meat begins to come away from the bone. Remove the hock and chicken. Cool the meat and the stock.

Cut the meat into small pieces and return to the stock, discarding the skin. Refrigerate. When the fat has congealed on top, remove the fat. Reheat soup and serve with cold garnishes, with wedge of lime added last to enhance the flavor. The addition of the lime is a *must*.

This serves 6 to 8 as a main course.

Pozole is a Mexican soup made of pork and hominy. This variation uses chicken as well.

Puree of Lima Bean Soup

2 packages (10 ounces each) frozen baby lima beans
3 cups chicken stock
2 egg yolks
1 cup heavy cream
2 tablespoons butter
salt and pepper to taste

Cook the lima beans covered in chicken stock in a large 2½-quart saucepan until they are tender. Puree them in a blender. Mix together the egg yolks and heavy cream. Warm this with a little of the puree mixture. Add to the puree and return to pan over low heat. Do not let boil after the eggs and cream have been added. Stir in butter and salt and pepper. Garnish with croutons and serve hot.

Serves 6 to 8.

Mrs. Flagler Matthews serves this soup to her guests at her midday Sunday dinner, a very traditional meal with lace tablecloth and fine silver.

Fresh Mushroom Soup

8 tablespoons butter
5 cups chopped green onions including green tops
1 teaspoon salt
½ teaspoon freshly ground pepper
2 tablespoons flour
5 cups chicken stock
¾ pound mushrooms

1¼ cups light cream
Topping—1 cup heavy cream whipped with ⅛ teaspoon salt and
cayenne to sprinkle.

In a heavy 2½-quart saucepan, soften butter. Add onions and
mix well. Place on stove burner and add salt and pepper. Cover
and cook very slowly for 10 minutes, being careful not to let
onions brown. Remove from heat and stir in the flour. When
smooth, add the stock. Return to heat and stir until the soup boils.
Let it simmer for 10 minutes, uncovered, then remove from heat
again. In the meantime wash and dry the mushrooms, and set
aside ¼ pound. Coarsely chop the remaining mushrooms and add
to the soup. Place contents in blender and blend until nearly
smooth. Return to pan and add cream. Heat until hot but not
boiling. Before serving, add the remaining mushrooms that have
been very thinly sliced. Top each serving with a dollop of whipped
cream and sprinkle of cayenne.
Serves 6 to 8.

*This soup freezes well if prepared up to the point of adding the reserved
mushrooms.*

Parsnip Soup

2½ tablespoons butter
4 medium onions, sliced
1 pound parsnips, scraped and cut into small pieces
1⅓ cups chicken broth
1⅓ cups water
salt and pepper
⅛ teaspoon curry powder
1 cup light cream
½ cup milk

In a 3-quart saucepan, melt the butter. Add the onions and cook
over low heat until soft and translucent. Add the parsnips, broth,
and water. Simmer covered until parsnips are tender. Add salt,
pepper, and curry powder. Blend in a blender until pureed. Return
to saucepan and add cream and milk. Serve hot or cold garnished
with parsley. If the soup thickens too much after chilling, thin with
more milk or broth.
Serves 6 to 8.

Mushroom Soup Citron

6 tablespoons butter
5 tablespoons flour
4 cups chicken stock
2 cups milk
1 pound mushrooms, coarsely chopped
2½ tablespoons lemon juice
1 cup heavy cream
salt and pepper to taste

Melt butter in a large 2½-quart saucepan. Add flour and cook slowly for 3 minutes, stirring constantly. Add stock, blending well with a wire whisk, and bring to a boil. Add milk, mushrooms and lemon juice. Cook for 5 minutes. Pour into a blender and blend for approximately 30 seconds till combined. Return to pan, adding cream, salt, and pepper. Serve hot or cold.
Serves 6 to 8.

Queen Victoria Green Pea Soup

1 pound shelled peas or 2 packages (10 ounces each) frozen peas
1 medium raw potato, sliced
1 medium onion, sliced
1 head iceburg lettuce, cut into wedges
2 cups heavy cream
4 cups chicken stock
few drops lemon juice
salt and pepper to taste

Place peas, potato, onion, lettuce, and half the stock in a large 2½-quart saucepan and bring to a boil. Cover and simmer for 20 minutes. Place the cooked vegetables and liquid into a blender and blend until pureed. Return to pan and add the remaining stock; simmer 5 minutes. Add cream and lemon juice and season to taste with salt and pepper. Serve hot or cold.
Serves 6 to 8.

Indian River Soup

1 can (16 ounces) plum tomatoes with basil, undrained
1 carrot, shredded

½ of one medium onion, chopped
½ bay leaf
rind of 1 lemon
6 peppercorns
3 cups clear chicken broth
2 tablespoons sugar
½ cup dry white vermouth
salt and freshly ground pepper (preferably white)
rind of one orange
juice of one orange
2 tablespoons finely chopped parsley

In a heavy 2-quart pan, bring the first 6 ingredients to a boil, then simmer very gently, covered, for 8 minutes. Strain carefully into a mixing bowl. Rinse the pot and return the tomato liquid to the clean pot; then add the chicken broth. Place over moderate heat and add the sugar and vermouth. Bring almost to the boiling point, but proceed cautiously as the soup can suddenly become very hot. Season with salt and freshly ground pepper.

Meanwhile peel the orange very carefully, removing only the rind and avoiding the white membrane. Cut the peel into very thin strips, ½ inch long. Set aside the peel to be used as a garnish and squeeze the orange, adding the juice to the soup. Reheat the soup gently. Ladle into bowls or soup plates and sprinkle with finely chopped parsley and orange rind, finely sliced into slivers.

Serves 6 to 8.

If served cold, try adding a shot of chilled vodka to each bowl.

Watercress Soup

3 tablespoons butter
⅓ cup minced onion
3 to 4 cups washed and dried watercress leaves and stems, roughly
    chopped
½ teaspoon salt
3 tablespoons flour
6 cups chicken stock
2 egg yolks
½ cup heavy cream
2 tablespoons butter

Melt butter in a large 2½-quart saucepan. Add onions and cook over low heat 5 to 10 minutes until tender but not browned. Stir in watercress and salt. Cook, covered, for 5 minutes or until leaves are wilted and tender. Sprinkle in the flour, stirring constantly over moderate heat for 3 minutes. Off the heat, beat in the stock. Return to heat and simmer for 5 minutes. Place contents in blender and puree. Return to saucepan. Blend the yolks and cream in a mixing bowl. Add 1 cup of hot soup in droplets to the yolks and cream. Slowly pour back into soup mixture. Add butter and stir over medium heat for 1 to 2 minutes. Do not simmer. Serve hot. If serving cold, omit butter.

Serves 6 to 8.

Cream of Zucchini Soup

2 pounds young green zucchini
4 tablespoons butter
4 tablespoons finely chopped shallots
3¼ cups chicken broth
2 cloves garlic, finely chopped
½ teaspoon salt
1 cup heavy cream
¼ teaspoon curry powder

Scrub zucchini. Do not peel. Slice thinly. In a heavy skillet, heat the butter and then add the zucchini, shallots, and garlic. Cover tightly and simmer 15 minutes, being careful not to let it brown. Spoon vegetable mixture into a blender, then add remaining ingredients and blend for about 30 seconds until smooth.

Serve hot with croutons or cold with chopped chives for garnish.
Serves 6 to 8.

Cream of Spinach Soup

2 packages (10 ounces each) frozen chopped spinach, cooked according to instructions and drained
3 cups chicken broth
3 small onions, chopped
4 tablespoons butter
3 tablespoons flour
2 cups light cream
2 egg yolks, slightly beaten

salt
pepper
nutmeg

Place cooked spinach in blender with 1 cup of the chicken broth and the chopped onions. Blend. Onions should retain slightly crunchy texture. Set aside.

In a small saucepan, melt the butter over medium heat. Add the flour and cook for 1 to 2 minutes, stirring constantly. Add the cream and remaining 2 cups broth, beating with a wire whisk until combined. Bring to a boil over medium heat and stir until slightly thickened and smooth. Mix 2 to 3 tablespoons of the hot cream sauce with the egg yolks in a small dish. Pour this egg mixture back into the cream sauce and stir over very low heat until blended, about 1 minute. Season with salt and pepper and nutmeg. Pour the cream sauce into blender with spinach and blend until all combined. Adjust seasoning. Serve hot or cold. When heating to serve hot, do not boil.

Serves 8.

James O'Sullivan's yacht, *Horizon. Mort Kaye Studios*

John Rybovich, Jr., builder of sport fishing boats, with Ernest Hemingway.

Fish and Seafood

The turquoise waters of the Atlantic Ocean and Lake Worth surround the island of Palm Beach, offering the opportunity for all types of water sports, game fishing, and just plain relaxation.

One family that literally lives on the water is the James O'Sullivans. Businessman Jim O'Sullivan, his artist wife, Loulie, and their two small children call home a ninety-two-foot yacht, *Horizon*, which is usually tied up at the Peruvian Avenue docks. When the O'Sullivans entertain for dinner in the handsome teak-paneled dining room, guests are seated at an oval glass-topped table in small velvet-covered chairs. The warmth of the home surroundings makes one forget the gentle rocking of the boat as traffic passes on the intracoastal waterway. Freshly caught snapper with cucumber stuffing* is one of the hostess's favorite entrées for her dinner parties.

The O'Sullivans enjoy asking a dozen or so friends to go boating with them for the day. They cast off late in the morning after making sure that the bar is well stocked with beer and Bloody Mary mix. All liquid refreshments are served in custom-designed white mugs with *Horizon* emblazoned on the side. These mugs, made from the material used in rocket nose cones, are heavy and virtually spillproof.

After trying many different kinds of food as good luncheon fare on the high seas, the *Horizon*'s specialty developed because of a misunderstanding. Loulie had asked her helper to arrange some meat and cheese on a platter with bread for sandwiches. The Norwegian man misunderstood her directions and produced instead a tray of beautiful open-faced sandwiches garnished with pickles and olives. These proved to be easier to serve and eat while under way than anything else Loulie had planned before. In addition to the sandwiches, a hot fish chowder or hot or cold Spanish consommé is often added to the menu—served in the nose-cone mugs, of course.

*Recipe on page 109.

Well-known sportsman Jim Kimberly likes to collect and read cookbooks, but mostly he likes to cook. Most of his serious cooking is done at his Gray Fox Farm on the eastern shore of Maryland. There in the huge warm kitchen he will tackle such projects as wild goose with chestnut dressing prepared from home-grown chestnuts that have been boiled, peeled, and chopped before being frozen. He has a penchant for Maryland seafood delicacies, and oysters prepared any way are his favorites. Jim Kimberly feels that relaxation and good conversation are the most important ingredients of a successful party, and an oyster roast provides a good atmosphere for both of these.

At his oyster roasts, he serves raw oysters on the half shell; roasted oysters with cocktail sauce, vinegar, or melted butter; great tureens of oyster stew; fried oysters; and scalloped oysters.*

Onion hushpuppies always accompany his oyster feasts.

For Kimberly's onion hushpuppies, he combines one cup of yellow cornmeal, one cup of all-purpose flour, two eggs, one cup of milk, one cup of chopped onion, and a pinch of salt, mixes all ingredients together and fries them by the spoonful in deep fat at 375°. Hushpuppies will float to the top when done.

A good old-fashioned beach party is a favorite of vivacious Lilly Fuller, who loves to combine guests of all ages in this informal atmosphere. With a full moon shining on a broad beach and the charcoal grills beginning to smoke, Lilly will welcome her guests with carafes of white wine and Sunshine Specials, a combination of champagne and orange juice. The dinner menu might include barbecued chicken, marinated fish,† creoled shrimp, or oyster casserole.** Her Southern background shows through in the choice of creole corn, eggplant casserole, or ratatouille as an accompaniment. Since Lilly loves to dance, she often arranges to have some kind of music after dinner. She finds that even if her teen-age children have other plans for dinner, they're quick to return for the dancing. "Music and champagne" pull a party together for Lilly Fuller whether the party is indoors or out.

John Rybovich is not only a blue-ribbon boat builder, but also an award-winning angler and founder of the prestigious light-tackle Masters Invitational Tournament. Sleek, custom-designed sport fishing boats have been handcrafted for two generations in the

*Recipe on page 107.
†Recipe on page 109.
**Recipe on page 108.

Rybovich boatyard on the shore of Lake Worth. John fishes for the table as well as for trophies, and he offers much sage advice on the cleaning, storing, and freezing of Florida's many saltwater fish. "Fish is the most fragile of foods and has to be treated with great care from the time it is taken aboard to the time it is served." For those who fish in warm waters like those of Florida, ice must be carried to store the catch. In John's estimation, ice is as important an ingredient for a good fishing trip as beer.

All fish skin is covered with a protective slime, and in the cleaning process cooks must be very careful not to let any of this bitter slime from the cutting board touch the delicate flesh. Fish should be washed vigorously before skinning, steaking, or filleting, but after the flesh is exposed, water for washing should be used sparingly, if at all.

Those fish which do *not* need to be skinned are mackerel, pompano, trout, some snappers, and wahoo. Mackerel and wahoo should be scraped thoroughly; pompano, trout, and snapper need to be scaled thoroughly, and this can be done more easily if the fish is kept wet. Dolphin, grouper, snook, cobia, bluefish, and some snappers must be skinned before filleting. For all other types John recommends that they be filleted first and then skinned.

John Rybovich stresses that in handling, cleaning, or packaging, the fillets should not be folded or crushed. If the fresh fish is to be used immediately, it should be filleted and placed flat in a covered shallow pan or in plastic wrap in the coldest part of the refrigerator. If the fish is to be frozen, it is best to package it in small containers so that only what is needed can be defrosted.

When freezing fish, start by prechilling in very salty ice water. If the fish is in fillets, wrap them while very wet in freezer paper, remembering to keep them flat; put as many as possible in a heavy plastic bag, and seal, taking care to store the bag on a flat surface. For portion-size pieces of a larger fish or fish surface. For portion-size pieces of a larger fish or fish steaks, start by prechilling, then put the pieces in small heavy bags, add enough saltwater to cover, squeeze any air out of the bag, and seal tightly against the fish. If the fish is going to be deep fried after defrosting, prepare in 1-inch cubes, prechill in cold salt water, and store in small plastic bags filled with salty water.

Small fish to be frozen whole should be cleaned thoroughly, except for pompano, which can be scraped clean without gutting, frozen whole, and filleted after defrosting. Oily fish such as pompano and mackerel do not freeze well for extended periods of time. For the best taste, frozen fish should be used within a month.

Like many other Florida fishermen, John Rybovich prefers to cook fish and shellfish quickly with a minimum of seasoning. He feels that long cooking trends to toughen the tender flesh, and heavy seasoning or sauce mask its delicate flavor. His favorite methods include broiling, baking in foil, and frying.

Broiling—for fillets or thin steaks ½ to ¾ inch thick.

Place fillets skin side down on waxed paper, squeeze sour citrus juice (lemon, lime, or sour orange, or calamondin) over them and allow to stand for 20 minutes. Season with salt, pepper, monosodium glutamate, and paprika. Transfer to a well-buttered piece of foil and broil 4 inches from heat until golden and flaky but still moist. Cooking time will depend on thickness of fillet or steak. A ½-inch fillet should require no longer than 5 minutes. Steaks should be turned over halfway through cooking, and pompano can be started skin side to the heat and turned when half cooked. Butter or garlic butter can be brushed on after 3 minutes.

Baking in foil—for small whole fish weighing about a pound.

Clean fish thoroughly by removing entrails, gills, and all fins that might puncture the foil. Make several slits in the skin on both sides and squeeze lemon, lime, or calamondin juice over and inside the fish. Season sparingly with salt, pepper, monosodium glutamate, and paprika. (In other methods of cooking some of the seasoning will burn away, but in foil cooking all the flavors are sealed in.)

Cut a piece of foil three times as long and twice as wide as the fish. Drain the fish by holding up by the head for a few seconds, then place in the center of the foil and add several thin slices of onion. If the fish is a dry-fleshed fish like snapper, add several pats of butter on top of the fish and in the ventral cavity. Bring the long edges of foil together and fold down in an interlocking flat seam to within 1 inch of fish. Fold in ends almost to the head and tail. Bake in preheated 400° oven for 50 minutes, turning package over after 30 minutes. Take care not to puncture the foil.

Frying Tempura-Style—for bite-sized pieces of firm fish and shellfish.

The success of this manner of frying depends on three things: maintaining the temperature of cooking fat at 375° to 400°, keeping the fish as cold as possible, and keeping the batter ice cold.

Combine 1 cup lemon or lime juice with ½ teaspoon each of salt, pepper, paprika, and monosodium glutamate. (If key limes are available, substitute ⅔ cup key lime juice and ⅓ cup orange or grapefruit juice.)

Marinate fish or shellfish in seasoned liquid in a well-sealed plastic bag in the refrigerator for 30 minutes. Turn over several times during this time, then drain. Marinate the fish several hours before serving, but only for a period of 30 minutes. A longer marination will actually begin to cook the fish, and the flavor of the marinade will become too dominant. Refrigerate the pieces of well-drained fish until ready to cook.

Fill bottom of double boiler with ice cubes and ice water. Immerse top of double boiler in ice water. Break 1 cold egg into measuring cup and add enough ice water to make ¾ cup. Pour into cold pan, beat lightly with a whisk, and stir in enough self-rising flour to make a batter the consistency of light cream.

Heat fat to 375° to 400°. Remove a few pieces of fish from refrigerator, dust with self-rising flour, coat with batter, and drop one at a time into fat, making sure temperature does not drop below 375°. Skim excess batter from top of fat with slotted spoon. Cook until golden, remove to hot dish lined with paper towels. Serve with tartar sauce as main course or appetizer.

Beachcomber Scampi

14 tablespoons butter
2 tablespoons flour
1 cup canned beef bouillon, undiluted
2 tablespoons sherry
4 tablespoons finely minced shallots
1 cup dry white wine
2 to 3 tablespoons lemon juice
2 tablespoons chopped fresh parsley
2 cloves garlic, crushed
salt and pepper
36 jumbo shrimp, deveined, but leaving tails and shells attached

Preheat oven to broil

Prepare brown sauce by melting 2 tablespoons of the butter in a small saucepan. Add the flour and cook over medium heat, stirring constantly, for 1 to 2 minutes. Pour in the bouillon, beating vigorously with a wire whisk until combined. Bring to a boil over medium heat, stirring. Remove from heat and add the sherry. Melt 4 tablespoons of the butter in a 1½-quart saucepan over medium heat. Add shallots and sauté about 1 minute. Add the white wine and reduce over medium heat to ⅓ of the original volume. Stir in the brown sauce and bring to a boil. Then remove from heat. Add the remaining 8 tablespoons (½ cup) butter, melted, the lemon juice, parsley, garlic, and salt and pepper to taste. Set aside while preparing shrimp.

Hold each shrimp so the underside is up. Slice down its length, almost to the vein, to form the hinge. Spread and flatten to form a butterfly shape. Set them in a large ovenproof platter or shallow casserole, with the flesh side up. Sprinkle lightly with salt, pepper, and paprika. Spoon the sauce evenly over the shrimp. Broil about 6 to 8 inches from the heat 7 to 8 minutes, basting once.

Serves 6 to 8.

Crabmeat Remick

2 pounds fresh crabmeat
12 slices bacon, cooked and crumbled
2 cups mayonnaise
1 cup chili sauce
2 teaspoons tarragon vinegar
2 teaspoons dry mustard
1 teaspoon paprika
½ teaspoon celery salt
dash of cayenne

Preheat oven to 350°.

Drain crabmeat and remove bony tissue. Divide equally between 8 buttered scallop shells or ramekins. Sprinkle with the crumbled bacon. Set shells in a large baking pan for easy handling. Heat for 5 minutes in oven while mixing the topping. In a bowl, blend the mayonnaise, chili sauce, vinegar, mustard, paprika, salt, and cayenne. Remove shells from oven and reset oven to broil. Spoon topping over the heated crabmeat. Broil 4 to 5 inches from the heat until hot and bubbly. This may be prepared in a 3-quart flat baking dish, if desired, following the same instructions.

Serves 6 to 8.

Small portions of Crabmeat Remick make an interesting first course.

Crab Ramekins

4 tablespoons butter
½ pound mushrooms, thinly sliced
2 pounds fresh crabmeat
4 tablespoons flour
2 cups milk
¼ cup dry white wine
2 tablespoons lemon juice
salt and white pepper
4 slices bread, cubed
2 tablespoons chopped fresh parsley
½ cup grated Swiss cheese
paprika

Preheat oven to 400°.

Melt 2 tablespoons of the butter in a skillet over medium heat. Add the mushrooms and sauté until the liquid has evaporated and they are lightly browned. Set aside. Drain crabmeat and remove any bony tissue. In a 1½-quart saucepan melt the remaining 2 tablespoons butter over medium heat. Add the flour and cook, stirring constantly, for 1 to 2 minutes. Pour in all at once the milk and wine, beating vigorously with a wire whisk, until combined. Bring to a boil over medium heat and cook until thick and smooth. Remove from heat and add lemon juice plus salt and white pepper to taste. Combine cream sauce with the crabmeat, sautéed mushrooms, bread cubes, and chopped parsley. Adjust seasonings. Divide among 8 buttered scallop shells or ramekins. Sprinkle the cheese on each shell and top with a sprinkle of paprika. Place shells on a large baking pan for easy handling and bake for 15 to 20 minutes or until bubbly and cheese melts.

Serves 6 to 8.

This may be prepared early in the day and refrigerated. Bring to room temperature and add cheese and paprika just before baking. Also a good first course in small servings.

Crabmeat Hollandaise

6 to 8 artichoke bottoms
6 tablespoons butter

1½ pounds crabmeat
1 egg, hard-boiled, and chopped fine
1 tablespoon lemon juice
dash Tabasco
salt
white pepper
1½ cups Hollandaise sauce (recipe p. 000)

Preheat oven to 450°.

If using canned artichoke bottoms, rinse under cold water and set in flat baking dish that has been buttered.

In a 1½-quart saucepan melt the butter over low heat. Add the crabmeat, egg, lemon juice, Tabasco, and salt and pepper to taste. Combine and heat thoroughly. Divide the mixture among the artichokes. Top the filled artichokes with the Hollandaise and set in the oven just until brown, approximately 2 to 4 minutes.

Hollandaise Sauce

3 egg yolks
12 tablespoons butter
1 tablespoon lemon juice
salt and pepper (white)

In a warmed bowl, mix the yolks thoroughly with a wire whisk. Do not beat to a froth.

Melt the butter in a heavy 1½-quart saucepan over moderately high heat. When it is foaming, pour it onto the egg yolks in a thin stream while beating vigorously with a wire whisk. If the yolks are warm and butter hot enough, there should be 1½ cups Hollandaise. Add the lemon juice and salt and pepper and beat until combined.

Serves 6 to 8.

Oyster Soufflé

2 pints fresh oysters
6 tablespoons butter
6 tablespoons flour
2 cups half and half cream
6 beaten egg yolks

salt and white pepper
⅛ teaspoon nutmeg
2 tablespoons lemon juice
6 egg whites

Preheat oven to 325°.

In a large, heavy saucepan, heat the oysters in their liquid over medium heat for a few minutes until they are plump, but the edges have not curled. Drain them, reserving the liquid.

Melt butter over medium heat in a heavy 1½-quart saucepan. Add the flour and cook, stirring constantly, 1 to 2 minutes. Pour in the half and half, beating vigorously with a wire whisk until blended. Stir until it comes to a boil and is smooth. Add ½ cup reserved oyster liquid, the oysters, nutmeg, and lemon juice. Reduce the heat to low and add the egg yolks. Stir over the heat for 1 minute to allow yolks to thicken. Season to taste with salt and pepper. Set aside to cool slightly.

Beat egg whites until stiff, but not dry. Fold gently into the cooled oyster mixture. Pour into an ungreased 2½-quart soufflé dish and bake 40 to 45 minutes until firm.

Serves 6 to 8.

The filling for this soufflé may be prepared early in the afternoon of the day to be served, and refrigerated. Remove from refrigerator, fold in whites, and bake as directed.

Jim Kimberly's Scalloped Oysters

3 cups prepared herb seasoned cube stuffing
1½ pints fresh oysters (stewing size)
salt and freshly ground pepper
½ cup light cream
½ cup liquid from the oysters
3 tablespoons butter.

Preheat oven to 400°.

Grease a 7 x 12 shallow casserole. Spread evenly over the bottom 1½ cup of the cube stuffing. Arrange the drained oysters on top and sprinkle with salt and pepper. Sprinkle with the remaining cubes over all. Combine the cream and oyster liquid and pour evenly over the casserole. Dot with the butter. Bake for 25 minutes, uncovered.

Serves 6 to 8.

Oyster Casserole

1 clove garlic, crushed
½ cup olive oil
¾ cup grated Parmesan cheese
½ cup cracker meal
½ teaspoon salt
¼ teaspoon pepper
1 quart select oysters, washed and drained
¼ cup sherry

Preheat oven to 450°.

In a bowl, place the garlic and olive oil. In another bowl, mix the cheese, cracker meal, salt and pepper, combining well. Dip each oyster in the oil and then coat with the cheese mixture. Arrange in a well-buttered 9 x 13 baking dish. Sprinkle with any remaining cheese mixture and also sprinkle the top with the sherry.

Bake 12 to 15 minutes, or until oysters are lightly browned. Serves 6 to 8.

Broiled Mackerel with Mango Chutney

8 fillets of mackerel, or any fresh fish
4 limes
salt and pepper
1 cup butter
2 cups of mango chutney

Preheat oven to broil.

Line 1 large or 2 medium-sized flat baking dishes with foil. Butter foil well and place fillets on top of foil, skin side down. Squeeze 1 lime, halved, over the fillets. Salt and pepper lightly and set aside. Melt the butter in a saucepan and add the chutney and juice from the remaining 3 limes.

Broil the fish 4 to 5 inches from the heating element for 3 to 4 minutes, then begin basting with the butter chutney mixture, being careful not to burn the mango. Broil while basting for another 5 to 10 minutes or until fish is tender.

Serves 6 to 8.

This may be prepared with any fresh fish by adjusting the broiling time if necessary. If desired, shaved, toasted almonds may be sprinkled over fillets during last minute of broiling.

Lilly Fuller's Marinated Fish

6 to 8 fish fillets, or enough fillets to total 3 pounds
¼ cup Worcestershire sauce
6 sprigs fresh dill, or ½ teaspoon dried dill
½ cup white wine
3 tablespoons butter
salt and pepper

Place fillets in a flat dish and add the Worcestershire sauce, dill, and wine. Cover and marinate in the refrigerator for 2 to 3 hours. Transfer fillets to a greased casserole. Dot with butter and salt and pepper to taste. Broil about 6 to 8 inches from the heat for 8 to 10 minutes.
Serves 6 to 8.

Horizon Stuffed Snapper

1 6-pound snapper, cleaned, with head and tail intact
garlic salt
freshly ground pepper
6 tablespoons butter
¼ cup finely chopped onion
5 cups small dried (overnight) bread cubes without crusts
1¼ cups chopped, seeded, and peeled cucumbers
2½ teaspoons chopped capers
pinch of ground cloves
1 teaspoon sage
⅓ cup toasted almonds, chopped
7 tablespoons dry white wine, divided
salt
pepper
2 slices bacon

Preheat oven to 350°
Rub whole fish inside and out with garlic salt and pepper. Set

aside. Melt butter in large, heavy skillet over medium heat. Add onions and sauté until soft but not brown. Remove from heat and add the bread cubes, cucumber, capers, cloves, sage, almonds, and 5 tablespoons of the wine, and mix well. Adjust seasoning to taste with salt and pepper. Stuff the prepared fish lightly. Place in shallow buttered baking dish and place the remaining stuffing underneath the fish. Sprinkle with the remaining 2 tablespoons of wine and place the bacon strips over the top. Bake for 30 to 45 minutes, uncovered, until flaky and moist.

Serves 6 to 8.

Sole Fantaisie

6 to 8 fillets of sole, or enough to total 3½ to 4 pounds
2 to 3 tablespoons lemon juice
salt and pepper
¾ pound shrimp, cooked, deveined, and cut in half
½ pound mushrooms, thinly sliced
½ pound shallots, finely chopped
2 cans (10 ounces each) condensed cream of celery soup, undiluted
2 tablespoons green Chartreuse
¼ cup grated Parmesan cheese

Preheat oven to 350°
Butter a baking pan, large enough to hold the fillets in one layer. Arrange fillets in pan. Sprinkle lemon juice over them and season with salt and pepper. Arrange the shrimp, mushrooms, and shallots over the fillets. Top with the soup that has been mixed with the Chartreuse. Bake 15 to 20 minutes. Remove from oven and sprinkle with cheese. Reset over to broil, and set fish under broiler until nicely browned.

Serves 6 to 8.

Baked Trout with Mushrooms

1 cup melted butter
1 pound mushrooms, sliced
8 trout
salt and pepper
flour
½ cup fine bread crumbs

110

4 scallions, minced
lemon

Preheat oven to 400°
Melt 3 tablespoons of the butter in a large heavy skillet over medium heat. Add the sliced mushrooms and sauté until the mushroom liquid has evaporated and they are lightly browned. Place in bottom of a large, flat, buttered baking dish large enough to hold the trout. Set aside.

Rinse and dry the trout. Dredge in flour that has been seasoned with salt and pepper. Melt ¼ cup of the butter in a large heavy skillet over moderately high heat and fry the trout, 2 or 3 at a time, for about 6 minutes on each side, until brown. Remove from skillet and continue with rest of fish in the same manner, using ¼ more cup of butter.

Place the trout over the mushrooms. Sprinkle with the bread crumbs that have been combined with 2 tablespoons of the melted butter. Bake for 15 minutes, uncovered. Meanwhile melt remaining 3 tablespoons of butter in a small skillet, and add scallions. Simmer for 1 minute. Pour over baked fish. Serve with lemon wedges.

Serves 6 to 8.

Sea trout, snapper, dolphin, sole, or any other similar fish may be substituted for the trout.

Cold Poached Trout

1 4-pound trout, boned with head reserved for stock
1 large onion, whole
2 celery stalks
2 medium carrots, cut into 1-inch pieces
2 to 3 sprigs of parsley
salt to taste
10 to 12 peppercorns
1 tablespoon white vinegar

Sauce:

¼ pound cooked and deveined shrimp, cut into 2 or 3 pieces
1 cup mayonnaise

3 tablespoons pickle relish
1 hard-boiled egg, chopped fine
1 tablespoon lemon juice
½ cup sour cream

Garnish:

1 bunch watercress, washed and dried
4 to 5 tomatoes, quartered
1 lemon, sliced
8 artichoke hearts
4 hard-boiled eggs, quartered

In a large fish poacher or large roasting pan, place enough water to cover the fish. To the water add the onion, celery, carrots, parsley, salt, peppercorns, and vinegar. Bring to a boil and add fish and the fish head. Reduce heat, cover, and simmer the fish. Cook the fish 10 minutes to each inch of thickness (measure from the thickest part of the fish). Carefully remove the fish from the poacher. Remove any skin and allow to cool. Chill. Combine all the sauce ingredients and chill.

Strain and freeze the fish stock for future use. When ready to serve, place fish on a large platter on a bed of watercress. Arrange the tomatoes, lemon, eggs, and artichokes around the fish and serve with sauce.

Serves 6 to 8.

Mrs. Samuel Rautbord likes to serve this fish on her cold buffet.

Coquille St. Jacques

1½ cups dry white wine
1 teaspoon salt
6 peppercorns
3 sprigs of parsley
1 small bay leaf
¼ teaspoon thyme
4 tablespoons chopped shallots
½ cup water
1½ pound bay scallops
7 tablespoons butter

½ pound mushrooms, very thinly sliced
¼ cup flour
¾ cup milk
3 egg yolks
½ cup heavy cream
1 teaspoon lemon juice
cayenne
½ cup grated Swiss cheese

Preheat oven to 400°.

In a heavy 2-quart saucepan combine wine, salt, peppercorns, parsley, bay leaf, thyme, shallots, and water. Bring to a boil, cover, and simmer over low heat for 5 minutes. Strain liquid, discarding herbs, then return to saucepan. Add scallops and simmer, covered, 5 more minutes. Remove scallops from liquid, then boil liquid down over high heat to 1 cup. Set aside. Melt 2 tablespoons butter in small skillet over medium heat and add mushrooms and sauté until all the liquid has evaporated and they are lightly browned, about 8 minutes. Set aside.

Melt 3 tablespoons butter in a 1-quart saucepan over medium heat. Add flour and cook, stirring constantly, for 1 to 2 minutes. Add milk and reduced 1 cup cooking liquid, beating vigorously with a wire whisk until combined. Over medium heat bring this to a boil, stirring constantly, until thick and smooth. In a separate bowl beat yolks and cream. Slowly return mixture to hot cream sauce. Cook over very low heat for 1 minute. Remove from heat. Add lemon juice, cayenne, scallops, and mushrooms. Adjust seasoning. Spoon mixture into 8 buttered shells or ramekins and sprinkle with cheese. Dot with remaining 2 tablespoons butter. Bake about 5 to 10 minutes until browned and bubbly.

Serves 6 to 8.

This may be prepared ahead of time and frozen up to 1 week in advance. Bring to room temperature and add cheese before baking. In smaller portions it may be used as a first course.

Seafood Quiche

3 tablespoons butter
2 tablespoons minced scallions, including tops

1½ cup cooked seafood, crabmeat, lobster, shrimp, or a combination
2 tablespoons Madeira or dry white wine
3 eggs, beaten
1 cup heavy cream
1 tablespoon tomato paste
½ teaspoon salt
dash pepper
1 9-inch pie crust
¼ cup grated Swiss cheese

Preheat oven to 375°.

Melt butter in a heavy skillet over medium heat. Add scallions and sauté until soft. Remove from heat and add seafood and wine. In a separate bowl mix eggs, cream, tomato paste, salt, and pepper until smooth. Combine with the seafood mixture. Pour into a prepared 9-inch pie crust and sprinkle with cheese. Bake about 30 minutes or until knife inserted in center comes out clean.

The crust and filling may be prepared early in the day and refrigerated separately. Remove from refrigerator 1 hour before assembling.

Serves 6. To serve 8, this recipe must be doubled, using 2 pie crusts.

Poultry

Lilly Rousseau is a popular Palm Beach hostess as well as a luminary in the fashion world with her famous Lilly Pulitzer dresses. She loves to entertain and has her own distinct philosophy about the subject. She wants to serve food that tastes good, is presentable and fun, but she'd rather her guests remember what a good time they had than what they ate. When she entertains, Lilly does all her own cooking, but she has plenty of kitchen help—her guests. Everyone finds his way there to chop or stir.

Saturday or Sunday lunch, Cuban-style, is her favorite time to entertain, since she is busy at work during the week. Friends who call on a weekend morning to find out if the Rousseaus are at home are cheerfully included in Lilly's luncheon plans. She and her husband, Enrique, love to spend the weekend mornings on their boat, but before leaving the docks, Lilly calls the market to order the groceries for lunch and tells the Mexican maid how many places to set. She returns home around noon and while friends swim and chat and wander in and out of the kitchen, Lilly creates a meal. What is in the refrigerator is her inspiration, and she rarely follows a recipe. "And, of course, it's black beans and something, or Enrique is in tears. Every Cuban has to have his black beans." Generally she has luncheon ready in about an hour so her guests can play cards in the afternoon.

On any given Saturday or Sunday there might be ten to thirty people for lunch in the sunny yellow frame house on the lake trail. It is a home that bursts with activity, color, and pets of every description. The center of the house is a marvelous kitchen that can seat eighteen plus an additional four at the snack bar. Lilly serves all her meals in a casual, buffet style in this warm, woodsy kitchen. Indeed at lunch there are no tablecloths or place mats. Guests put their colorful plates on the bare wooden table.

115

The kitchen of Lilly Pulitzer Rousseau features two refrigerators and two dishwashers. The long refectory table she uses for dining can be glimpsed in the corner of the picture. *Jack Maitland*

One of Lilly's favorite menus includes tangy baked chicken* that has an interesting crispy texture created by coating the pieces in crumbled potato chips before oven frying. With this chicken dish she serves rice, black beans†, and avocado and onion salad. Her traditional Cuban dessert is canned guava shells and cream cheese with Cuban crackers. A cool pitcher of Sangria accompanies luncheon. Lilly does everything very naturally—especially entertaining. She blends many different kinds of people, good food, and a casual atmosphere with a relaxed hostess, and the combination works!

A Palm Beacher whose name has long been associated with a discriminating taste for good food is Mrs. Augustine Healy. Among her many credits is that of teaching cooking classes at Au Bon Gout, an interesting Worth Avenue store that is now a shopping club. Her fifteen years of teaching firmly established her culinary reputation in the area, and her pupils have included such notables as Jacqueline Kennedy Onassis.

Harriet Healy has two kitchens in her beautiful home. The one in the back of the house that functions as her workshop is a French country-style room with warm woods and exquisite china. Often when Mrs. Healy invites four or six for luncheon they begin with a soup course served in the living room. A homemade chicken broth flavored with clam juice, with whipped cream on top and presented in pot de crème cups is one of her favorites. After the soup she and her guests retreat to her kitchen haven for the main course. She feels that Chicken Au Bon Gout,** a unique combination of ground white chicken and ground beef served with a sauce made of onions and rice, makes an exciting luncheon dish. With this she chooses tomatoes provençale as a vegetable and a fruit for dessert.

For a casual lunch Mrs. Healy often serves soup and a sandwich, but since so many of her friends are weight conscious, she prepares her sandwich in a special way. She slices protein bread in half horizontally after toasting it to make two very thin slices. This makes a thin, crisp sandwich. For melba toast she spreads the slices with Clarified Butter,†† retoasts them, and keeps them in an airtight jar where they can be stored for several days. Clarified butter does not burn as quickly as regular butter. She buys several

*Recipe on page 121.   **Recipe on page 118.
†Recipe on page 181.   ††Recipe on page 126.

117

pounds of butter, clarifies it by melting it, places it in the refrigerator overnight, removes all milky substance in the morning, and washes it under the tap in the sink. Then it can be refrigerated or frozen.

Chicken Au Bon Gout

1¾ cup cream
breasts of 6 chickens, boned, skinned, and cut into small pieces
1 small onion or shallot, peeled
2 slices white bread with crusts removed, crumbled
½ pound twice-ground round steak
1 egg
2½ teaspoons salt
⅛ teaspoon pepper
4 tablespoons butter
Lemon Parsley Butter or 8 mushroom slices

Preheat oven to 350°
Place in a blender ½ cup cream, ½ of the chicken pieces, and the onion. Blend, using the on-off technique, and loosen meat mixture around blades with a long rubber spatula. Remove to a bowl and repeat with remaining chicken pieces and ½ cup cream. Add to bowl. In a separate bowl soak the bread in ¾ cup cream. Add ground round and bread to the chicken mixture. Stir in egg, salt, and pepper and beat by hand until light and fluffy. Chill 2 hours or more. Beat again. Melt butter in large skillet. With wet hands quickly mold the chicken mixture into patties and drop into hot butter. Sear quickly on both sides but do not overbrown. Reduce heat and cook slowly for 20 minutes, turning twice. Serve with a small ball of Lemon Parsley Butter or a mushroom slice on top of each pattie.
Serves 6 to 8.

Lemon Parsley Butter

¼ cup butter, softened
1 tablespoon finely chopped fresh parsley
1 teaspoon lemon juice
salt to taste

118

Cream all the ingredients together and divide into 6 to 8 portions to be placed on patties of Chicken Au Bon Gout.

Harriet Healy recommends using a food processor when preparing the chicken since this can be heavy work for the average blender. She assembles the patties a day ahead, refrigerates them, and sautées them just before serving. She places them on a serving platter and with a pastry tube pipes a Soubise Sauce (see following recipe) around the edges.

Soubise Sauce

3 tablespoons butter
1 large Bermuda onion, chopped
1 cup cooked rice
1¼ cups chicken broth
6 mushrooms
1 egg yolk
4 tablespoons cream
sprig of parsley
salt and pepper to taste

In a medium saucepan, melt the butter and sauté the onion until translucent, being careful not to brown it. Add the cooked rice and chicken broth. Bring to a boil and simmer gently for 5 minutes. While this is cooking, place the mushrooms in a small saucepan with enough water to cover and cook 5 to 10 minutes until tender. In a blender combine the rice mixture, the drained mushrooms, the egg yolk, cream, and parsley. Blend until smooth. Add salt and pepper to taste. Keep warm in the top of a double boiler over simmering water until ready to serve.

Capon With Sauce Supreme

1 capon (about 6½ pounds), dressed and trussed
2 stalks celery with leaves
12 peppercorns
1 leek, trimmed
4 sprigs parsley
1 bay leaf
3 sprigs thyme or 1½ teaspoons dried

1 teaspoon salt
1 onion, peeled
1 carrot, scraped
5 tablespoons sweet butter
4 tablespoons flour
1 cup heavy cream
2 egg yolks
1 teaspoon lemon juice

Place the capon in a large saucepan or kettle and add the celery and peppercorns.

Cut the leek down the center almost to the base of the root. Wash the leek carefully under running water. Add it to the saucepan along with the parsley, bay leaf, thyme, salt, onion, and carrot. Add water to cover. Bring to a boil, then simmer, partially covered, for about 2 hours. Prick the joint between the thigh and drumstick with a fork. When the juice runs clear, remove the capon and keep warm. Skim off fat from the stock. Reduce the stock by about half, over high heat; strain and reserve.

Melt 4 tablespoons of the butter in a saucepan and stir in the flour until blended. Add 4 cups of the reserved stock, stirring vigorously with a whisk. Simmer gently until thickened, approximately 30 minutes.

Return capon to the remaining stock in the kettle to keep it hot and moist.

Just before serving, complete sauce. In a small bowl, beat the egg yolks into the cream. Add a small amount of the hot cream sauce and stir. Add this mixture to remaining hot cream sauce and cook over low heat, stirring 1 to 2 minutes. Add the lemon juice and remaining tablespoon of butter. Correct the seasoning. Cut the capon into serving pieces; place on a warm serving dish. Spoon a little of the sauce over each piece and serve the remaining sauce separately.

Serves 6 to 8.

Moore-Betty Chicken

2 roasting chickens (2½ to 3 pounds each)
coarse salt
2 cloves garlic
freshly ground pepper

6 tablespoons lemon juice
1 cup water

Preheat oven to 400°.

Wipe inside of chickens with damp cloth or paper towel, and sprinkle very generously with coarse salt. Peel garlic clove. Rub salted insides of chickens with cut garlic. Make a very thorough job of this so that the garlic rubs off on the salt. Dust with freshly ground pepper. Rub a generous tablespoon of coarse salt into chicken skins, followed up with the cut clove of garlic. Truss or tie up the chickens for the oven and stand them on a rack in a roasting pan.

Pour half of lemon juice inside the chickens and the remainder over them. Dust with a little more coarse salt and freshly ground black pepper. Pour water into bottom of roasting pan. Cook for 1 hour without basting.

Serves 6 to 8.

The coarse salt is a vital ingredient since it seals in the moisture during cooking. Serve this chicken hot or cold. The carcass makes a convenient base for making chicken stock.

Lilly Pulitzer's Baked Chicken

1 cup juice from lemons, limes, or sour oranges
1 teaspoon salt
1 teaspoon freshly ground black pepper
1½ cups dry white wine
6 cloves garlic, crushed
1 teaspoon basil
3 broiler chickens, quartered
1 cup melted butter
3 cups crumbled potato chips

Preheat oven to 400°.

In a large bowl, combine juice, salt, pepper, wine, garlic, and basil. Add chicken pieces, cover, and marinate in refrigerator for 4 hours, turning occasionally. Remove chicken pieces and pat dry. Dip each piece into the melted butter and then roll in the crumbled chips. Arrange pieces in a large, flat, buttered baking dish and bake uncovered for 1 hour.

Serves 6 to 8.

Mrs. Enrique Rousseau uses this recipe when serving a crowd and adds black beans and rice to the menu.

Crab-Stuffed Chicken

4 tablespoons butter
¼ cup flour
¾ cup milk
¾ cup chicken stock
⅓ cup dry white wine
¼ cup chopped onion
¾ pound crabmeat
¼ pound mushrooms, chopped
½ cup (10) crumbled saltine crackers
2 tablespoons parsley
½ teaspoon salt
dash of pepper
breasts of 4 chickens (12 ounces each) halved, boned, skinned, and
    flattened between two sheets of waxed paper with a cleaver to 8 x
    5 x ⅛ inches
1 cup (4 ounces) shredded Swiss cheese
½ teaspoon paprika

Preheat oven to 350°.
Melt 3 tablespoons of the butter in a 1½-quart saucepan and add flour. Cook over low heat 2 to 3 minutes, stirring constantly. Add milk, stock, and wine and beat vigorously with a wire whisk to blend, and cook until it boils. Simmer 2 to 3 minutes longer, stirring until it thickens. Melt remaining 1 tablespoon of butter in a small skillet and sauté onion in it until soft. Stir in the crabmeat, mushrooms, crackers, parsley, salt, and pepper. Blend in 2 tablespoons of the sauce. Top each chicken piece with ¼ cup mixture, fold in the sides, and roll up. Place seam side down in 12 x 7 x 2 dish. Pour remaining sauce over all. Bake covered for 1 hour. Remove from oven and sprinkle with cheese and paprika and bake a few minutes longer.
Serves 6 to 8.

The stuffed breasts and sauce may be prepared in advance and refrigerated separately, then brought to room temperature before assembling and baking.

Chicken à la Grecque

breasts of 5 chickens, halved and boned
2 cups milk
¼ teaspoon white pepper
4 tablespoons butter
½ cup olive oil
1½ cups chopped onion
1 cup sauterne
1 cup green seedless grapes
1 cup pitted black olives
1 teaspoon chopped mint
1 teaspoon chervil
dash of salt
dash of garlic salt
dash of white pepper

Preheat oven to 325°.
Soak chicken breasts in milk seasoned with pepper for several hours. Melt butter and olive oil in large heavy skillet and add onion. Sauté over medium heat until lightly browned. Remove onion with slotted spoon and set aside. Drain the chicken and brown quickly over high heat in the butter and oil remaining in the skillet. Transfer to a heatproof casserole and add the browned onions, sauterne, grapes and olives, mint, chervil, salt, pepper, and garlic salt. Bake uncovered for 1 hour.
Serves 6 to 8.

This can be assembled hours ahead of time and then baked as directed.

Chicken Alaska

13 tablespoons butter
7 tablespoons flour
2 cups milk
1⅛ cup chicken stock
⅞ cup dry white wine
¼ teaspoon salt
dash nutmeg
1 pound cooked lobster meat, cut into small pieces

123

breasts of 6 or 7 chickens, halved, boned, and skinned
¼ cup freshly grated Parmesan cheese

Preheat oven to broil.

Melt 5 tablespoons butter in heavy 2-quart saucepan. Add the flour and cook over low heat 2 to 3 minutes, stirring constantly. Pour in the milk, stock, and wine all at once, beating vigorously with a wire whisk. Continue beating until smooth and boiling, then cook over medium heat, stirring until thickened. Add the salt and nutmeg, check for seasoning. Add the lobster meat and set aside.

Melt 4 tablespoons butter in a heavy skillet and add enough chicken breasts to comfortably cover the bottom. Sauté them on both sides until lightly browned, taking approximately 8 minutes. Remove cooked breasts to a large casserole or gratin dish large enough so they make only one layer. Sauté the rest of the breasts in the same manner, using more butter if necessary. Remove to casserole. Pour lobster sauce over chicken and sprinkle with cheese. Brown under broiler.

Serves 6 to 8.

This combination of chicken and lobster is a special recipe of Phil Romano, whose restaurants are well known in the Palm Beaches. The chicken and sauce may be prepared ahead of time and refrigerated separately. Assemble in casserole, bake 15 to 20 minutes in preheated 350° oven. Brown under broiler.

Rolled Chicken Washington

2 tablespoons butter
¼ pound mushrooms, finely chopped
2 tablespoons flour
½ cup light cream
¼ teaspoon salt
dash cayenne
1¼ cups shredded sharp cheese
breasts of 6 chickens (12 ounces each), halved, boned, skinned,
    and flattened between two pieces of wax paper with a cleaver to
    8 x 5 x ⅛ inches.
flour

2 eggs, slightly beaten
¾ cup fine dry bread crumbs

Preheat over to 325°.
Melt butter in a small skillet and add mushrooms. Sauté over medium heat for 5 minutes. Sprinkle 2 tablespoons flour over the mushrooms and blend well; stir in the cream. Add the salt and cayenne. Cook over medium heat, stirring, until mixture becomes very thick. Add cheese and stir over very low heat only until cheese melts. Turn mixture into an 8 x 8 x 2 cake pan, cover, and chill thoroughly (about 1 hour). Cut the firm cheese mixture into 12 equal portions, shaping them into short sticks.
Sprinkle the flattened breasts with salt and pepper. Place a cheese stick on each chicken breast. Fold over the sides and roll up the breast, being sure no cheese is visible. Press to seal well. Dust the rolls with flour, dip into the eggs, then roll in the bread crumbs. Cover and chill thoroughly at least 1 hour. Deep fry the rolls in hot fat (375°) about 5 minutes, until golden brown and crisp. Drain on paper towels. Place rolls in shallow baking dish and bake 30 minutes.
Serves 6 to 8.

This may be prepared ahead of time up to the baking and frozen. Bring to room temperature and proceed as directed.

Honeymoon Chicken

salt and pepper
breasts of 4 chickens, halved, boned, skinned, and flattened with a
  cleaver between two sheets of waxed paper
½ cup Clarified Butter (recipe page 126)
2 tablespoons sherry or vermouth
2 teaspoons freshly grated lemon rind
2 tablespoons lemon juice
1 cup heavy cream
8 thin pats of butter
¼ cup grated Parmesan cheese

Preheat over to broil.

Salt and pepper the chicken pieces. In a heavy skillet melt Clarified Butter, and add some of the chicken pieces in one layer.

Sauté them over moderate heat 5 to 8 minutes, turning once to cook both sides. Remove cooked pieces to a flat casserole or gratin dish large enough to hold all the chicken in a single layer. Repeat until all chicken pieces are cooked. Put wine, lemon rind, and juice into remaining butter in skillet and cook, stirring for 1 minute over low heat. Add cream slowly and cook, stirring constantly over moderate heat 3 to 5 minutes. Salt and pepper to taste. Pour sauce over chicken. Place a pat of butter on each piece of chicken, sprinkle over all with cheese, and broil until lightly browned.

Serves 6 to 8.

The chicken and sauce may be combined and refrigerated in advance. Bring to room temperature and bake in 350° oven for 15 to 20 minutes. Add butter pats and cheese and broil as directed.

Clarified Butter

Clarified Butter is melted butter with the sediment removed. Since the milky particles in ordinary butter blacken first when butter is heated, the clear, yellow, clarified butter burns less easily.

To clarify butter cut into pieces and melt in a saucepan over low heat. Remove from heat and let stand a few minutes, allowing the milk solids to settle to the bottom. Skim the butterfat from the top and strain the clear yellow liquid into a container. The residue may be stirred into soups or sauces as an enrichment.

Chicken and Biscuits

1 cup butter or margarine
breasts of 6 chickens, halved, boned, with skin left on and tucked under to make a neat square bundle, using a toothpick if necessary
½ to ¾ cup flour
1 tablespoon paprika
2 teaspoons thyme
salt and pepper to taste
1 cup butter or margarine
10 unbaked biscuits

Garnish:

½ pound mushrooms, quartered
2 tablespoons butter

Preheat oven to 400°.
Melt butter in the bottom of a 9 x 13 roasting pan and set aside ¼ cup of it. Dust the chicken bundles well with the flour to which the paprika, thyme, salt, and pepper have been added. Place them, skin side down, in the roasting pan with melted butter. Drizzle the reserved butter over the top. Bake 35 minutes. Remove breasts and toothpicks and place on heated platter skin side up. Keep warm. Place uncooked biscuits on top of remaining butter in pan and bake 10 to 12 minutes or until done. Meanwhile melt 2 tablespoons butter in small skillet and sauté mushrooms until lightly browned. Remove baked biscuits with spatula and arrange around chicken, pouring the remaining butter over the chicken. Garnish with mushrooms.
Serves 6 to 8

A recipe for Biscuits follows. Packaged refrigerated biscuits may be substituted.

Biscuits

2 cups sifted all-purpose flour
4 teaspoons baking powder
1 teaspoon salt
¾ cup sweet butter
½ cup milk
1 egg mixed with 1 tablespoon water to glaze

Preheat oven to 450°.
Into a bowl, sift flour, baking powder, and salt. Cut the butter into the dry ingredients. Add milk, mixing lightly with a fork until the flour binds. Roll the dough to approximately 1 inch thick. Cut with a small biscuit cutter. Brush with glaze and bake 10 to 15 minutes.
Makes 24 biscuits, 1½ inches in diameter.

Entrance to Mr. and Mrs. Guilford Dudley's house, which was designed by
Addison Mizner, *Mort Kaye Studios*

Game

Visitors who think of Palm Beach only as a narrow ribbon of land that borders the Atlantic Ocean are often surprised at the availability of game in this large county, which extends from Jupiter south to Boca Raton and west into the Glades. There are hundreds of acres of public hunting preserves in the area, and many Palm Beach residents lease hunting rights from landowners in the county. Hunters bring home quail, dove, duck, turkey, wild pig, and deer for bountiful eating.

One Palm Beach hostess who enjoys fixing game herself is Mrs. Guilford Dudley.* The Dudleys are from Nashville, Tennessee, and make their winter home in a stately Mizner house that has a magnificent living room with a view of both the lake and the ocean. Jane Dudley entertains in the same manner whether she is in Palm Beach or Nashville or Denmark, where they lived when her husband was ambassador. She favors a seated dinner and feels that small parties are apt to be the most memorable. For her the most important ingredient of any successful party is the guest list. She enjoys giving parties with a special theme or for a particular occasion and remembers particularly the luncheon she and her husband gave honoring the American astronauts and Russian cosmonauts who met in space. For this occasion she chose regional dishes and planned her decorations with a wildlife theme. The centerpieces were loose arrangements of wild flowers, lilies, and grasses.

When *Field and Stream* executive editor Al McClane and his wife, Patti, decided to give a game dinner in their Palm Beach home, they ended up having 500 guests and serving them buffet style in a circus tent set up on their lawn. The huge and aptly titled menu featured such treats as hogs (one was cooking in the coals while the other was being carved), and buffalo steaks were cooked to order. Al and Patti had fixed the goose livers and the venison†

*Recipe on page 131.
†Recipe on page 133.

themselves the night before, and these and several other items needed only to be heated before serving. Just to read the menu which they sent with the invitations is enough to whet the appetite!

THE GROANING BOARD

Buffalo Jerky
made by Indian Ben

Iron Gate Red Salmon Caviar
for Poor Young Men

Wyoming Elk Salami
from Wind River

Everglades Venison Beaujolais
with Mushrooms aux Fines Herbes
Winnipeg Goldeye steamed in Banana Leaves

North Carolina Mountain Pig on the Coals

Roast Haunch of Buffalo kept from Willows

Liver of Hudson Bay Snow Geese in Cognac
with Truffles

Smoked Dakota Pheasant

Buffalo Rib Steaks
as done by Cheyenne Indians

Florida Rock Shrimp Sauté

Smoked Spey River Salmon

Gulf Mullet Smoked in Sweet Bay

Garlicked Red Peppers and Swamp Cabbage

Potatoes Vinaigrette a la Hamner

Conchiglie

Varies

Imported Cheese

Salads
Fruits

Dudley's Dove

12 doves, cleaned
salt and pepper
flour
6 tablespoons butter
1 cup chopped celery
1 cup chopped onion
2 cups beef consommé
½ cup red wine

Preheat oven to 350°.
Season doves with salt and pepper. Dust with the flour. In a large, heavy skillet, melt the butter. Add the dove and brown slowly on all sides over medium heat. Transfer to a large casserole. Add the celery, onion, and consommé to the casserole. Cover and bake for 2 hours. During the last ½ hour of cooking time, add the red wine.
Serves 6 to 8.

Kentucky Quail

8 tablespoons butter
16 to 24 quail, cleaned and left whole
½ cup bourbon, warmed
½ cup sherry
salt and pepper to taste
1 cup chicken stock
2 cups heavy cream

In a large, heavy skillet or casserole over moderately high heat, melt 4 tablespoons of the butter. Place 7 or 8 quail in melted butter,

being sure they do not touch. Brown well on all sides. Set aside browned quail and brown remaining birds in the same manner, using the remaining 4 tablespoons butter. After all the quail are browned, return them to skillet or casserole and pour in warm bourbon and sherry. Ignite. When flame burns out, salt and pepper the birds well and add the stock. Cover and simmer over low heat slowly for 20 minutes. When birds are tender, add cream and simmer 5 more minutes, uncovered. Adjust seasonings.
Serves 6 to 8.

This may be prepared ahead of time up to adding the cream and frozen, if desired. When ready to serve, bring to room temperature. Bring to simmer over medium heat, add the cream, and proceed as directed.

Pheasant

6 young pheasant, hung for 4 days and cleaned
12 strips bacon
salt and pepper
¼ teaspoon thyme
¼ teaspoon powdered juniper berry
¼ teaspoon nutmeg
¼ teaspoon clove
1 cup port wine
½ cup chicken broth
3 inches celery root, grated
2 tablespoons parsley
1 bay leaf
2 tablespoons grated onion
¾ cup red currant jelly

Preheat oven to broil, then to 325°.
Split each pheasant in two and broil on a well-greased rack for 3 minutes on each side. Line a large baking pan with the raw bacon. Set the bird halves on top of the bacon. Season them with salt and pepper, thyme, juniper berry, nutmeg, and clove. Pour the port wine and chicken broth over the birds. Sprinkle over the top the grated celery root, parsley, bay leaf, and grated onion. Cover with a sheet of buttered paper and bake for 40 minutes. Remove the paper after 30 minutes and baste frequently for the last 10 minutes.

Gravy: Strain the pan juices through a sieve into a saucepan and taste for seasoning. Stir in the currant jelly and bring to a boil, stirring until jelly is dissolved.

Serve the birds on a platter and the sauce separately.

Serves 6 to 8.

McClane's Venison

4 pounds venison (fillet preferred), cut into 1-to-1½-inch cubes or fingers
1 cup olive oil
1 cup vegetable oil
3 tablespoons soy sauce
2 to 3 tablespoons lemon juice
1 tablespoon seasoned salt
1 tablespoon paprika
2 garlic cloves, crushed
1 tablespoon meat tenderizer (only if a tough cut of venison is used)
2 tablespoons dried tarragon
1 cup white wine
¼ pound melted butter

Preheat over to 250°.

Place venison in a nonmetallic bowl. In a separate bowl mix thoroughly the oil, soy sauce, lemon juice, salt, paprika, garlic, tenderizer, and tarragon. Pour over meat and marinate covered in refrigerator for 8 hours or overnight. Remove meat and reserve marinade. Scatter the pieces of meat on the grid of the barbecue grill over low heat. Baste frequently with marinade for approximately 20 minutes. Drippings will smoke and to some extent flame; both are desirable in the flavor and cooking. Transfer venison to a large, shallow baking dish and add the wine and melted butter. Set in oven for 15 minutes.

Serves 6 to 8.

This is one of the McClanes' favorite venison recipes. Their accompaniment is wild rice with a dollop of black currant jam.

The home of Mrs. Andrew A. Fraser. *Mort Kaye Studios*

Beef

"The feeling of friendship is like that of being comfortably filled with roast beef." This eighteenth-century sentiment attributed to Samuel Johnson, no doubt expressed after he had finished an exemplary meal, is close to the hearts of beef lovers of all ages. Mrs. Andrew Fraser regularly plans her menu around beef when she entertains eight to twelve people for a seated dinner. "I'm careful not to go exotic unless I know my guests very well." She feels that both the Florida climate and avid weight-watching make people content to eat less, so if she serves a soup course she is careful to avoid having rich hors d'oeuvres. She frequently selects seafood, particularly crabmeat, as a first course, and she tries to create an eye-appealing combination of the meat and vegetables which follow.

Helen Fraser feels that "the interest of the hostess makes a good party." She takes considerable care planning the details of the menu and the seating arrangement since she believes that a party that isn't planned won't be successful. She particularly likes giving a dinner party for people who are alone on Christmas night, since that time of year can be sad for single people or those without family or houseguests. Each guest receives a small gift which the hostess has wrapped, and all take part in carol singing after dinner. "I love Christmas because it's corny. You don't have to be chic," she admits.

One Palm Beach restaurateur likes to have a large standing rib roast of beef* for a festive dinner at home, and the leftovers are served for dinner the following evening. The beef retains its moist quality and even its rareness after its first serving if it is wrapped in lettuce leaves and brown paper, stored in a cool place but not refrigerated, and warmed in a slow oven before serving for the second time.

*Recipe on page 136.

Roast Beef

1 rib roast beef (4 to 6 pounds)
salt and pepper to taste

Preheat oven to 500°.

Rub beef with salt and pepper. For very rare meat cook for 5 minutes per pound at 500°. Keep the oven door closed while cooking. When meat has cooked the allotted time, turn off the oven. Leave the meat in the oven to rest for at least 2 hours. It can wait up to 4 hours. Do not open the oven door during this time. For medium rare roast beef, add 5 minutes to the total cooking time before turning the oven off. For medium roast beef, add 10 minutes to the cooking time.

Serves 6 to 8.

Beef cooked this way will wait for all latecomers.

Steak Diane

2 tablespoons plus 1½ cups butter
8 thin boneless minute steaks, pounded
1½ cups chopped scallions or shallots
1 teaspoon salt
2 teaspoons ground pepper
1 cup red wine
2 teaspoons Dijon-style mustard
1 teaspoon Worcestershire sauce
⅔ cup warmed cognac

In the 2 tablespoons of butter sear the steaks on both sides a few at a time. Roll loosely and keep warm on a heated platter.

In a large, heavy skillet melt 1½ cups butter. Add the scallions or shallots and sauté lightly. Add salt and pepper, wine, mustard, and Worcestershire sauce. Cook for 2 minutes. Add steaks and baste with the sauce. Pour in cognac, ignite, and cook 1 to 2 minutes longer or until done to personal preference. Serve, pouring sauce over steaks. If a somewhat thicker sauce is preferred, boil down to desired consistency.

Serves 6 to 8.

This is a nice dish to prepare for an intimate dinner party.

Lobster Stuffed Tenderloin of Beef

4 to 6 pounds whole beef tenderloin
2 lobster tails (4 ounces each)
1 tablespoon butter, melted, plus ½ cup butter
1½ teaspoons lemon juice
6 slices of bacon, partially cooked
½ cup sliced scallions
½ cup butter
½ cup dry white wine
⅛ teaspoon crushed garlic
¼ pound whole mushrooms
5 sprigs watercress

Preheat oven to 425°.
Cut tenderloin lengthwise to within ½ inch of bottom to butterfly. Place lobster tails in boiling salted water just to cover. Return to boiling; reduce heat and simmer 5 to 6 minutes. Carefully remove lobster from shells. Cut lobsters in half lengthwise. Place lobster, end to end, inside beef. Combine 1 tablespoon melted butter and lemon juice. Drizzle on lobster. Close meat around lobster; tie roast together securely with string at intervals of 1 inch. Place on rack in shallow roasting pan. Roast for 20 minutes for rare doneness. Lay bacon slices atop; roast for 5 minutes more.
Meanwhile, in saucepan, cook scallions in remaining butter over very low heat until tender, stirring frequently. Add wine and crushed garlic and heat through, stirring frequently.
To serve, slice roast, spoon on wine sauce. Garnish platter with whole mushrooms and watercress.
Serves 6 to 8.

Truffled Tournedos

8 artichoke bottoms
¾ cup port wine
3 tablespoons butter
8 tournedos of beef
¼ cup brandy
salt and pepper to taste
8 truffle slices (or 8 mushroom slices)
8 tomato halves, grilled
16 asparagus tips, boiled

In a saucepan, warm artichoke bottoms in ½ cup of the port wine. Brown tournedos in butter on both sides in large frying pan. Add brandy and remaining ¼ cup wine and flame. Cover and simmer for 5 minutes. Season with salt and pepper. Serve tournedos on drained artichoke bottoms topped with a slice of truffle (or mushroom). To garnish, use grilled tomatoes and boiled green asparagus tips. Pour the gravy from the cooking pan over the tournedos.

Serves 6 to 8.

Beef Bourguignon

½ pound fat salt pork
16 to 20 small white onions, cooked
4 pounds lean beef (chuck), cut into 2-inch chunks
3 tablespoons flour
6 to 8 peppercorns, crushed
2 bay leaves
4 sprigs parsley
½ teaspoon thyme
½ teaspoon marjoram
¾ pound fresh mushrooms
1 tablespoon butter
2 to 3 cups dry red wine
salt to taste
finely chopped parsley

Preheat oven to 300°.

Slice the salt pork into ¼-inch slices and then into pieces about 2 x 1 inches. In a large, heavy, deep pot brown the pork until crisp. Remove pork, leaving the fat. Sauté the onions in the fat until lightly brown and remove. Sauté the meat in the same fat until lightly brown. Take off the fire. Put back the salt pork bits, shake the flour and crushed peppercorns over the meat, and lightly toss to blend flour. Add the bouquet garni of bay leaves, parsley, thyme, and marjoram. In a large skillet sauté the mushrooms in the butter over high heat. Add any juice from the skillet to the meat and reserve mushrooms. Add enough red wine to barely cover the meat. Bake uncovered for 3 to 4 hours until tender. Add salt to taste. About ½ hour before serving transfer the meat to an ovenproof serving dish. Place onions around the outside edge of the meat and the mushrooms in the center. Put back in oven to heat the onions and mushrooms thoroughly. Sprinkle with chopped parsley and serve.

Serves 6 to 8.

Carbonnade à la Flamande

4 pounds lean beef cut into 1-by-2-inch chunks
½ cup flour
½ cup cooking oil
2 pounds large onions, thickly sliced
6 cloves garlic, crushed
2 cans (10½ ounces each) beef broth
3 tablespoons brown sugar
¼ cup wine vinegar
½ cup chopped parsley
2 small bay leaves
2 teaspoons thyme
1 tablespoon salt
freshly ground pepper
24 ounces beer

Dumplings:

1 cup sifted all-purpose flour
2 teaspoons baking powder
½ teaspoon salt
3 tablespoons butter
1 egg, beaten
2 tablespoons chopped parsley
½ to ⅔ cup milk

Preheat oven to 325°.

Toss beef pieces lightly in flour. In a large skillet, heat the oil and brown meat a few pieces at a time. Remove to a large ovenproof casserole and repeat until all meat is browned. Brown onions and garlic in the skillet and remove to casserole. Pour off any oil left in the skillet, add the broth, and heat, stirring to loosen the brown bits. Pour over the meat. Stir in the sugar, 2 tablespoons of the vinegar, parsley, bay leaves, thyme, salt, and pepper. Stir in the beer. Cover the casserole and bake 2 hours. Transfer to top of stove and add remaining vinegar. Cook over medium heat until sauce bubbles.

Meanwhile prepare the dumplings. Combine flour, baking powder, and salt. Cut in butter with pastry blender or two knives. Combine egg, parsley, and ½ cup milk and stir into flour to make a soft dough, adding more milk if necessary. Drop dumpling batter by soup spoonfuls on top of bubbling stew, cover, and reduce heat. Steam gently 15 minutes.

Serves 6 to 8.

Carbonnade is a Belgian dish traditionally made with beer. It makes a hearty meal.

Beef Pignolia

¼ cup olive oil
1 clove garlic, crushed
1 large onion, peeled and sliced
1 green pepper, cut into thin long strips
2 pounds beef steak
¾ cup pignolias (pine nuts)
1½ teaspoons salt
¼ teaspoon pepper
½ tablespoon flour
½ cup beef bouillon
4 tablespoons dry sherry

Heat the oil in a large skillet. Add the garlic, onion, and green pepper. Slowly sauté for 3 minutes. Remove with slotted spoon and reserve. Cut the steak into bite-sized strips. Combine the beef and nuts and sauté in the skillet for 3 minutes over high heat until brown. Stir in the seasonings and the flour. Stir in the reserved onion mixture and gradually add the bouillon and sherry. Cook, stirring, until it boils. Simmer 5 minutes.

Serves 6 to 8.

The unusual feature of this dish is the contrasting textures of the chewy pine nuts and the crisp green pepper. It freezes well.

Boiled Beef with Horseradish Sauce

3 quarts water
1 quart beef bouillon
2 onions, sliced
2 carrots, sliced but not scraped
1 stalk celery, sliced
3 sprigs parsley
5 peppercorns
½ teaspoon salt
3 pounds brisket of beef

Horseradish Sauce:
½ cup whipping cream
½ cup grated horseradish (fresh, if possible)
1 teaspoon vinegar
½ teaspoon Dijon-style mustard

Bring the water and bouillon to a boil in a large, heavy pot. Add the rest of the ingredients except the beef and simmer for 1 hour. Return the stock to a full boil. Plunge in the brisket. Return to a boil and skim the top of the stock. Reduce heat, cover the pot, leaving just enough room for the steam to escape, and simmer 2½ to 3 hours or until fork tender. Salt and pepper to taste. Whip the cream for the sauce until stiff. Add the remaining ingredients. If using fresh horseradish, grate and add just before serving to prevent discoloration. If using bottled horseradish, this sauce may be made earlier in the day and refrigerated.

At her Austrian party Mrs. William T. Young, Jr., served this traditional favorite on a marble slab on the buffet.

Outdoor dining at the home of Mr. and Mrs. Philip Hulitar. *Mort Kaye Studios*

Veal

"Veal is the luxury meat of the affluent and the gourmet. It is preferred by the health-conscious and can be easily and simply prepared." This is the opinion of Geraldine Pucillo, a marvelous hostess in her own home, whose husband, Gus, is the chef and owner of Petite Marmite Restaurant. Petite Marmite has been a gastronomical landmark on Worth Avenue since it opened in 1949. It has received many national awards for its cuisine, but perhaps the supreme compliment was paid to its owner when the late Henri Soule, founder of Pavillon and La Côte Basque in New York, told Gus Pucillo, "I wish to buy your restaurant since you are getting all my customers."

Gus Pucillo believes that affluent people who used to eat beef almost exclusively are now becoming concerned with cholesterol levels and are changing their eating habits. His observation is that the knowledgeable now eat veal as many as three times a week, chicken or fish three times, and beef only once.

Geraldine Pucillo has also observed a definite change in the life-style of most Palm Beachers during the last twenty-five years. Even though the town still has more private chefs than any other place in the United States, there are not as many as before. People are selling their enormous homes and moving into smaller condominiums. Now many hostesses who used to have large houses and staffs will entertain in a private room at Petite for forty or fifty friends. When the Duke of Windsor was alive, the Duke and Duchess used to entertain at Petite Marmite. One season they gave a series of four dinner parties on consecutive nights, each time inviting four guests to the same table with the same menu and flowers.

Mrs. Pucillo's suggestion to the hostess is to organize her shopping and cooking. Make ahead at leisure and then freeze the basic chicken and fish stocks and brown sauce. For the cost-conscious hostess entertaining a large group, Mrs. Pucillo suggests having an appetizer buffet as a first course followed by a seated dinner where the entrée is passed. She feels that a buffet with several entrée selections is a very uneconomical way to entertain.

Mr. and Mrs. Philip Hulitar love to cook, and they enjoy doing it together. One will chop and peel while the other cooks, and their results are sensational. The Hulitars grow herbs at their oceanside home as well as tomatoes, radishes, and Italian lettuce that find their way into varied menus, often planned around a veal entrée.

Philip Hulitar was a prominent dress designer for thirty years, and now he puts his creativity to work both in cooking and in redecorating old houses. The Hulitars' preference for informal entertaining influences their plans for the houses they refurbish. They definitely feel that dining rooms are no longer practical, so when they entertain they use their loggia set with round tables for six or eight. The table settings are very important to Philip Hulitar's artistic eye, and the couple has collected unusual china and glassware from all over the world so that menus and table settings will be closely coordinated.

Scaloppine à la Marsala

2 pounds veal scallops, pounded paper thin
salt and pepper
flour
8 tablespoons butter
4 tablespoons olive oil
1 cup dry Marsala
1½ cups chicken stock
¼ pound mushrooms, sliced
2 tablespoons chopped fresh parsley

Season the veal with salt and pepper and dust with flour. Melt 4 tablespoons butter with 4 tablespoons olive oil in a 12-inch skillet. After foam subsides, add veal and brown quickly on both sides. Transfer to warm plate. Pour off most of the fat, leaving just a film in the skillet. Add Marsala and ½ cup chicken stock. Boil for 2 minutes. Return veal to skillet, cover, and simmer over low heat 10 to 12 minutes. Baste veal once or twice with pan juices. Remove cooked veal to heated platter. Add remaining chicken stock to skillet and simmer 4 to 5 minutes. When sauce is reduced, remove from heat and add 4 tablespoons butter. Add mushrooms and cook 1 to 2 minutes. Pour sauce over veal and sprinkle with parsley. Serves 6 to 8.

Veal Portofino

4 slices firm white bread
2 cups light cream
2 pounds lean veal, ground 3 times
6 tablespoons chopped chives
5 teaspoons salt
1 tablespoon dry tarragon
¼ teaspoon black pepper
2 eggs
8 slices mozzarella cheese
8 slices prosciutto ham
4 tablespoons Clarified Butter (recipe page 126)

Sauce:
3 tablespoons flour
2 tablespoons butter
2 cups chicken stock
1 tablespoon beef extract
3 tablespoons Madeira
chopped parsley to garnish

Crumble bread slices into cream and set aside. In a large mixing bowl combine veal, chives, salt, tarragon, and pepper. Add eggs and beat well. Add the bread to the meat mixture and beat well with a wooden spoon. Refrigerate for 1 hour or more. When ready to sauté, remove from refrigerator and beat again until light and fluffy. Wet hands and shape into 16 patties. Between sheets of waxed paper flatten each patty very thin. Place a slice of cheese and a slice of prosciutto on top of 8 of the patties. Cover with the remaining patties and pinch edges together. Using 2 large heavy skillets, melt the Clarified Butter over high heat and brown the patties on both sides. Lower heat to medium and cook 10 to 15 minutes longer.

While veal cooks, prepare the sauce by melting butter in 1½-quart saucepan. Add flour and stir well. Add stock, beef extract, and Madeira.

Arrange the veal on a hot serving platter and pour the sauce over all. Garnish with chopped parsley.

Serves 6 to 8.

Osso Buco

4 tablespoons butter
1½ cups finely chopped onion
½ cup finely chopped carrot
½ cup finely chopped celery
1 teaspoon finely chopped garlic
6 to 7 pounds veal shank or shin, sawed into 8 pieces, 2½ inches
    long and each tied with string
salt and pepper to taste
flour
½ cup olive oil
1 cup dry white wine
¾ cup beef or chicken stock
½ teaspoon dried basil
½ teaspoon dried thyme
3 cups fresh or drained canned whole tomatoes, coarsely chopped
6 sprigs parsley
2 bay leaves

Gremolata: (for garnish)

1 tablespoon grated lemon peel
1 teaspoon finely chopped garlic
3 tablespoons finely chopped parsley

Preheat oven to 350°.

In a heavy casserole, melt butter over high heat. When foam subsides add onions, carrots, celery, and garlic. Cook 5 to 10 minutes or until vegetables are lightly colored. Remove from heat. Season veal with salt and pepper and roll in flour. Heat 6 tablespoons olive oil in another heavy skillet until a haze forms. Brown veal over moderately high heat 4 to 5 pieces at a time, adding more oil as needed. Transfer veal to the casserole, placing pieces side by side over vegetables. Pour out oil in skillet, leaving just a film, and pour in wine. Boil until reduced to ½ cup. Stir in the stock, basil, thyme, tomatoes, parsley, and bay leaves, return to a boil and pour over veal. Add additional stock, if necessary, to half-cover meat. Bring to a boil, cover, and bake in lower third of oven, basting occasionally, for 1 hour and 15 minutes or until meat is tender. Remove veal to serving dish, ladle vegetables and sauce over it, and garnish with the Gremolata made by combining the lemon rind, garlic, and parsley.

Serves 6 to 8.

Blanquette de Veau

1 large onion, studded with 2 cloves
¼ cup chopped carrots
1 bay leaf
1 sprig thyme
2 sprigs parsley
4 peppercorns
2 teaspoons salt
1 quart boiling water
2 pounds stewing veal, cut into 2-inch pieces
12 small onions
5 tablespoons butter
¼ pound mushrooms, sliced
¼ cup flour
2 tablespoons lemon juice
2 egg yolks, slightly beaten
1 tablespoon chopped parsley

Prepare bouquet garni by tying the onion, carrots, herbs, and peppercorns in a piece of cheesecloth. Add salt to water. Simmer the veal and bouquet garni in the salted water 1 hour or more until meat is tender. Drain veal, reserving stock. Drop the small onions into a pan of boiling water for 1 minute, drain, and remove their skins when cool enough to handle. Sauté the onions gently in 2 tablespoons butter until golden. Cook the mushrooms in a double boiler with a little of the veal stock for 5 minutes or until tender. In a 1½-quart saucepan, melt the remaining 3 tablespoons butter, stir in flour, and when well-blended, add 3 cups of strained stock. Cook over medium heat, stirring constantly until mixture thickens and boils. Add lemon juice to slightly beaten egg yolks. Stir in a little of the hot sauce, return to remaining hot mixture, add veal and parsley and reheat. Serve on a hot platter with onions and mushrooms.

Serves 6 to 8.

Young veal is fine-grained and light in color. Older veal is darker in color and can be tough or stringy. Maurice Moore-Betty suggests that older veal be treated in this manner: Cover with cold water, add 2 tablespoons salt, and bring to a boil. Boil for 1 minute. Drain and rinse. Proceed as recipe directs.

Lamb

Palm Beach has a chapter of the prestigious Confrérie des Chevaliers du Tastevin, an international society of connoisseurs of wine and food whose history dates back two and one-half centuries. Twice a year the Chevaliers meet in black tie to savor an epicurean dinner. Recently, for a meeting of the Confrérie, the chef at the Breakers Hotel prepared a Carré d'Agneau Roti Edward VII, a dish created by the famed Escoffier during a visit by King Edward to the Ritz Hotel in Paris.

The lamb is prepared by completely boning the rack from underneath in such a way as to leave the skin intact. It is seasoned inside and stuffed with a fine truffled fois gras that has been marinated in Marsala wine. After the reshaped rack is wrapped in muslin and refrigerated for several hours, it is unwrapped and roasted with some mirepoix (diced celery, carrot, onion, and garlic) at 375° for about 30 minutes. It is basted during that time with Marsala and veal fond (light veal gravy). The cooking liquid is reduced by half, strained, and served over the rack.

Lamb can be used in robust peasant dishes as well as the classical Escoffier manner. Mrs. Alva Cuddeback chooses to serve lamb in an interesting French cassoulet when she entertains informally in her Mizner apartment overlooking Worth Avenue. Her traditional Cassoulet* combines lamb, pork, duck, and Bolisoor French sausage with white beans in a hearty one-dish meal that she feels is perfect for buffet service when space is as limited as hers. The kitchen in her apartment is so small that during large parties she stacks the dirty dishes in the bathtub of the guest bathroom next to the kitchen.

To keep appetites sharp for the filling cassoulet, Eloise Cuddeback eliminates any first course and serves crusty French bread and potted shrimp with the main dish. The tiny shrimp have been

*Recipe on page 153.

The garden room of Mrs. Alva Cuddeback's apartment, which was built by Addison Mizner. *Mort Kaye Studios*

soaked in vermouth, sautéed in clarified butter with garlic, and chilled. Another good accompaniment for cassoulet is a platter of thinly sliced tomatoes seasoned with onion, salt, garlic salt, and chopped parsley. Mrs. Cuddeback covers the platter with plastic wrap and refrigerates it for several hours so the tomatoes develop a dressing of their own juices. A crisp green salad and salad plates are at one end of the buffet, as well as a large piece of creamy Brie. Guests may have salad with the entrée or may take salad and cheese after the main course in the European manner. Fresh fruits are used for a centerpiece, and these are also for nibbling. A hearty red wine accompanies the meal.

Noisettes of lamb are a favorite of some hostesses who have help in the kitchen, as that particular cut can be quickly prepared while the first course is being eaten. Other hostesses who plan to fix the meat course on the outdoor grill choose a Rack of Lamb or a butterflied leg of lamb,* either of which can easily be prepared in the oven if a sudden shower should appear.

Rack of Lamb

6 tablespoons olive oil
6 tablespoons bread crumbs
2 tablespoons freshly chopped parsley
2 teaspoons oregano
2 teaspoons finely minced shallots
1 teaspoon crushed garlic
1 teaspoon salt
2 racks of lamb (3 to 4 pounds each)
pepper

Preheat oven to 450°.
In a bowl combine the oil, crumbs, parsley, oregano, shallots, garlic, and salt until well blended. Set aside. Place the racks of lamb, bone side down, on a rack in a roasting pan. Salt and pepper lightly. Roast for 20 minutes. Remove from oven and spread herb mixture evenly over the skinned side, dividing it between the two racks. Set back in oven for 10 more minutes for rare.
Serves 6 to 8.

*Recipe on page 165.

This rack of lamb can also be prepared on the barbecue grill. Have the butcher saw the chine bone between the chops for easier carving.

Fassolia Me Arni

2 cups dried white lima beans
2 tablespoons olive oil
1½ cups chopped onions
2 pounds lamb, cubed
2 teaspoons salt
½ teaspoon fresh pepper
1 bay leaf
1½ cups chopped tomatoes
2 tablespoons chopped parsley
3 cloves garlic, minced

Cover the beans with water. Bring to a boil. Cook for 5 minutes. Remove from heat and let stand for 1 hour. Drain off water; add fresh water to cover, bring to a boil and simmer 1½ hours. Drain and reserve 1½ cups of the liquid. In a heavy Dutch oven heat the oil and brown the onions in it. Add lamb and cook until brown. Add beans, reserved bean liquid, and seasonings. Cover and cook 1 hour over low heat. Add tomatoes and garlic. Cook until beans and lamb are tender, 1 to 1½ hours more.
Serves 6 to 8.

Navarin d'Agneau

3 pounds lean lamb shoulder, cut into serving pieces
3 tablespoons olive oil
1 tablespoon sugar
salt and freshly ground pepper
3 tablespoons flour
2 to 3 cups lamb stock or beef bouillon
2 tomatoes, peeled and chopped
2 cloves garlic, finely minced
¼ teaspoon thyme
1 bay leaf
12 small potatoes, peeled
6 carrots, scraped and cut into 1½-inch lengths
6 small turnips, peeled

12 small onions
1 cup shelled peas or 1 package frozen peas
1 cup green beans, cut into ½-inch lengths.

Preheat oven to 325°.
Brown the meat on all sides, a few pieces at a time, in oil. Transfer to a heavy heatproof casserole. Sprinkle meat with sugar and place over moderately high heat for 4 to 5 minutes. Season meat with salt and pepper, sprinkle with flour, and cook for 5 minutes longer, stirring. Add lamb or beef stock to cover. Add tomatoes, garlic, thyme, and bay leaf and bring to boil. Cover and bake in oven 1 to 1½ hours until the meat is almost tender. Skim off excess fat. Add potatoes, carrots, turnips, and onions. Cover and bake for 25 minutes or until vegetables are almost tender. Add the peas and green beans and bake for 10 minutes longer. If frozen vegetables are used, add them only for the last 5 minutes. Serves 6 to 8.

Cassoulet

2 pounds Great Northern white beans, soaked overnight in enough water to cover
4 ounces salt pork
1 large onion studded with 2 cloves
2 carrots, scraped and quartered
Bouquet garni of 3 sprigs parsley, 1 bay leaf, ½ teaspoon thyme, and 4 peppercorns, all tied in a cheesecloth
1 tablespoon butter
2 onions, chopped
2 cloves garlic, minced
1 can (15 ounces) tomato sauce
1 cup white wine
1 leg of lamb (5 to 6 pounds)
1 chicken or duck (3 to 3½ pounds)
1 pork roast (any kind, 4 to 5 pounds)
1½ pounds French or Polish sausage
salt and pepper
1½ cups bread crumbs
¼ cup chopped parsley
beef broth

Preheat oven to 350°.

Drain the soaked beans. Return them to a large kettle and cover them with fresh water. In a small saucepan, place the salt pork. Cover it with water and boil for 10 minutes. Drain and dice finely. To the beans, add the diced salt pork, the onion, carrots, and bouquet garni. Simmer gently until tender, 1 to 1½ hours. When the beans are tender, remove the bouquet garni, onion, and carrots. In a small saucepan, melt the butter and sauté the onions and garlic until soft. Add the tomato sauce and white wine. Stir until combined and add this to the cooked beans. Set aside.

Place the lamb, chicken, and pork on roasting pans and roast, removing each meat as it is cooked. Remove the meat from the bones and cut into large chunks. Place in a large bowl and set aside. In a large skillet, brown and gently cook the sausage in a small amount of water, covered. Drain, slice, and set aside.

In a deep, large casserole, repeat in layers the bean mixture, the assorted meats, and the sausage slices, ending with the beans. Salt and pepper lightly each layer. Top with the bread crumbs and parsley. Bring slowly to a boil on top of stove. Then place in oven, uncovered, for 1 hour. If the mixture seems dry, add broth. As it cooks, crack the crust several times.

Serves 12 to 14.

This may be prepared ahead of time before bringing to a boil on top of the stove. A wonderful buffet dish which tempts guests to dig down beneath the surface for all the tasty ingredients!

Pork

A succulent pork roast browned and crisp on the outside and moist on the inside is a mouth-watering treat either for family fare or special entertaining. Pork is a particular favorite of Cuban-born Mrs. Alfonso Fanjul, who enjoys serving a whole loin of roast pork at her Sunday family lunches. In the summer luncheon is served around the pool, and her large family and guests enjoy a swim before eating the traditional Cuban meal of roast pork, applesauce, fried banana chips, black beans, and rice and eggs en gelée among other items.

Lillian Fanjul enjoys inviting guests of all ages to her parties, and finds it an interesting challenge to make up compatible seating arrangements. For large parties, she prominently displays a seating chart in the room where guests are having cocktails so that everyone will mingle and not spend the beginning of the night engrossed in conversation with a future dinner partner. Mrs. Fanjul plans her menus to include some French, some American, and some Cuban dishes and likes to combine a cold first course such as a fish mousse with a hot entrée or reverses the order and serves a hot fish course with a cold entrée such as boeuf en gelée. At small, seated dinners the courses are passed, but for larger parties the first course is placed on the table and the main course is presented on a buffet. Even men who generally dislike buffets enjoy going to the Fanjul home, as each lady is requested in Cuban style to serve the gentleman on her right from the buffet before serving herself.

Mrs. William E. Buckley occasionally serves pork stuffed with prunes at her dinner parties. She orders a center cut of a loin of pork boned and with a pocket the length of the piece of meat. The pocket is stuffed with the prunes, the roast is re-formed, tied with a string, and cooked on top of the stove.* The fruit helps to keep the

*Recipe on page 160.

155

Dining room of Mr. and Mrs. Alfonso Fanjul. *Mort Kaye Studios*

The dining room of Mr. and Mrs. William E. Buckley. *Mort Kaye Studios*

pork moist and when the meat is sliced, the stuffing resembles a piece of truffle in each serving. Garnished with miniature oranges and crisp watercress, the roast is served on a Chinese Export platter.

Virginia Buckley's favorite number of guests for a dinner party is eighteen, and she adds two round tables for six to her dining table in the loggia. The Italian lucite and chrome chairs used with the round tables fold flat and can be stored in a closet when not in use. For centerpieces she often uses chrome containers filled with dried and bleached fern to which she has the florist add rhubrum lilies, orchids, or gerber daisies, dependng on the season.

Hungarian Pork Roast

4 tablespoons lard or vegetable shortening
1 loin of pork roast (4 pounds boneless or 6 pounds bone-in)
¾ cup finely chopped onion
¾ cup diced carrots, in ½-inch dice
1 teaspoon sweet Hungarian paprika
1 cup chicken or beef stock
salt to taste
freshly ground black pepper
2 tablespoons flour
1 cup sour cream
1 tablespoon finely chopped parsley
1 teaspoon capers, drained, dried, and chopped
1 tablespoon caraway seeds

Preheat oven to 350°.
In a 4-quart casserole, heat lard or shortening until a light haze forms over it. Add the pork and brown on all sides over high heat, 10 to 15 minutes. Remove meat, set aside, and reduce heat. Pour off all but a thin film of the fat. Add the onion. Cook over medium heat 8 minutes or until lightly colored. Add the carrots and cook 2 or 3 minutes longer. Turn off heat and stir in paprika. Continue to stir until vegetables are coated. Pour in the stock and return to heat, bringing to a boil. Stir any bits that cling to pan. Return pork to the pan, fat side up. Salt and pepper to taste and bring liquid to a boil again. Cover tightly and braise the pork in the middle of the oven for 1½ hours or until thoroughly cooked and tender. Baste it

occasionally with the pan juices while cooking. Transfer the pork to a heated platter. Pour the contents of the pan into a sieve set over a saucepan, pressing down hard on the vegetables before discarding them. Skim off as much as possible of the surface fat from the pan liquid and bring the sauce to a simmer on top of the stove. With a wire whisk beat the flour and sour cream together in a bowl and add to the mixture in the pan. Bring to a simmer again and add parsley, capers, and caraway seeds. Taste for seasoning. Carve the pork into ¼- or ½-inch slices and serve with sauce poured over them.

Serves 6 to 8.

Filet de Porc Sauvage

2 pork shoulder butts (3 pounds each with all visible fat removed and tied as nearly as possible into sausage shape)

Marinade:

2 cups red wine (Bordeaux or Burgundy)
⅓ cup chopped onion
1 clove garlic, crushed
1 bay leaf
2 tablespoons salt
5 twists of black pepper mill
¼ cup finely chopped carrot
¼ cup finely chopped celery
¼ teaspoon sage
1 tablespoon oil (used for searing pork)

Preheat oven to 350°.

Mix marinade ingredients. Wipe pork rolls with paper towels and place in glass or enamel container just large enough to hold them. Coat meat with marinade. Turn rolls every half hour for 3 to 4 hours or put dish in refrigerator overnight. Remove from refrigerator 5 or 6 hours before cooking time. Remove pork from marinade and wipe dry. Heat 1 tablespoon oil in a heavy skillet and brown pork on all sides. Place both pieces in ovenproof dish with a tight-fitting lid. The dish should be just large enough to hold the meat. Strain the marinade over the meat. Cover and place in the oven to cook for 2 hours. Serve with the sauce from the casserole.

Serves 6 to 8.

Mushroom-Stuffed Pork Chops

1½ pounds mushrooms
¾ cup butter
6 tablespoons finely chopped fresh parsley
1½ tablespoons finely chopped garlic
salt and pepper to taste
8 rib pork chops (1½ inches thick) with pockets

Preheat oven to 350°.
Sauté mushroom caps and stems in butter on both sides just till tender. Remove from pan and mince finely. Return to the remaining butter in the skillet and blend with parsley, garlic, and salt and pepper to taste. Spoon the mixture into the pockets in the chops, packing well. If necessary, secure them with toothpicks. Bake in a shallow dish for one hour.
Serves 8.

Southern Shredded Pork

3½ pounds fresh pork
2 tablespoons margarine
⅔ cup chopped onion
¼ cup vinegar
2 tablespoons brown sugar
1 cup catsup
¼ cup water
3 tablespoons Worcestershire sauce
1 teaspoon prepared mustard
2 teaspoons salt

Place pork in a large pot and cover with water. Bring to a boil. Reduce to simmer and cook until tender and easy to shred (approximately 1 to 1½ hours). Remove from water and pull meat apart, discarding all fat. To prepare sauce, in a saucepan melt the margarine. Add onion and brown slightly. Add other ingredients and simmer until blended. Add shredded pork, then simmer 15 to 20 minutes. Serve on buns or as a main course over rice.
Serves 6 to 8.

Beef may be used instead of pork. Substitute 3 ½ pounds stew beef and treat in same manner. Served in buns, this is a great item for a teen party.

Loin of Pork with Prunes

20 prunes, pitted
1 loin of pork (4 to 5 pounds), boned with a deep pocket cut the
length of the roast
hot water
2 teaspoons salt
½ teaspoon white pepper
¼ teaspoon powdered ginger

Cover the prunes with hot water and soak 30 minutes. Drain, reserving the liquid. Stuff the pocket in the pork with the prunes. Season the meat with the salt, pepper, and ginger and tie it with string. In a Dutch oven, brown the meat on all sides, cover, and cook over low heat until tender, about 1½ hours, basting occasionally with the pan juices. Serve the meat sliced with the strained pan juices.
Serves 6 to 8.

Mrs. William E. Buckley chooses this Swedish recipe because the pork is kept moist by the prunes and the sliced meat has an interesting truffled design.

Alfresco Grilling

Outdoor cooking or barbecuing is an integral part of South Florida living. For informal entertaining on balmy tropical nights, the gas or charcoal grill has become an essential. Whether the grill is located in the garden, patio, or pool area, it becomes an object of keen interest as guests gather around to watch the chef at work.

Mr. and Mrs. Jack Nicklaus, who live in Lost Tree Village, love the outdoor life-style of Florida. "Jack wanted to live in a place where he could play golf in the winter, and we both wanted a great place to raise the kids," Barbara Nicklaus recalls. Their sunny house is designed to open to the outdoors and to the pool and grass tennis court, which overlook Lake Worth. They had a gas grill built into the breakfast room adjacent to the kitchen so that the whole family, even the children, can use it conveniently. Barbara Nicklaus will often start steaks in the oven, and then her husband will finish them on the grill. They find it an easy way to entertain in a comfortable informal manner.

Morton Downey first came to Palm Beach when he appeared in Ziegfeld's *Palm Beach Nights*, and he revisited the town for many seasons before making his home here. When the Downeys entertain informally at their Everglades Island home, the host enjoys cooking his specialties on a gas grill. A butterflied leg of lamb is one of his favorites.

The Downey marinade for lamb is a combination of Japanese teriyaki sauce, garlic powder, seasoned salt, and pepper. Since Ann and Morton Downey like their lamb pink, he cooks the meat for 18 minutes over a high heat with the hood closed. The meat isn't sliced until a moment before serving. Often Morton will undercook the lamb on the outside grill and finish it up on the grill in the kitchen.

One of Mrs. Joseph Kennedy's favorites when she dines at the Downeys' is grilled filleted tenderloin of beef that has been

161

Mr. and Mrs. Jack Nicklaus entertain outdoors. *Merrill Green*

marinated in teriyaki sauce, chopped onions, and freshly ground black pepper. For this particular dish Morton prefers choice-grade meat rather than prime since he feels that choice is more flavorful.

Mr. William E. Hutton III enjoys entertaining very informally. Because he has a very limited amount of time to get ready for a dinner party, Willie will prepare a vegetable and a salad shortly before his guests arrive, and then grill the meat while he visits with his friends. Sometimes on weekends he will make up a batch of a terrific barbecue sauce, an original creation. He mixes it by taste; it has no recipe. It's a combination of about a hundred ingredients including Worcestershire sauce, barbecue sauce, butter, catsup, garlic, and spices.

He uses this sauce on chops, steaks, and hamburgers. "Willie burgers" are a popular Sunday-night treat, and he attributes the juicy finished product to the fact that he buys ground beef with a high fat content for outdoor grilling.

Vegetables also take on an added zest when prepared out-of-doors. Whole unpeeled onion with a covering of firm brown skin are easily cooked on the grill. They should be soaked for 30 minutes in salted water and then placed on the hot grill and turned several times for 45 to 60 minutes. Their charred appearance belies the hot creamy interior when they are fork-tender. Many vegetables can be grilled in individual packages of heavy-duty foil. Several whole mushrooms folded in a square of foil with a pat of butter, salt, pepper, and a few fresh tarragon leaves will cook on the grill in about 8 minutes. The foil package makes a convenient single serving dish. Unpeeled wedges or slices of tomato, seasoned with salt, pepper, and fresh basil, and folded in individual foil package servings take about 20 minutes over the hot coals.

Some of the recipes in this section can be prepared in a conventional broiler, but alfresco grilling gives them that special flavor.

Skewered Shrimp

½ cup olive oil
½ cup soy sauce
¼ cup lime juice
2 to 3 shakes garlic salt
1 tablespoon barbecue sauce
freshly ground pepper

36 to 40 large shrimp, shelled and deveined
20 to 24 mushrooms
6 firm medium tomatoes, quartered

In a large bowl, combine oil, soy sauce, lime juice, garlic salt, barbecue sauce, and pepper. Add shrimp and marinate, covered, in the refrigerator for at least 2 hours. On each skewer alternate 4 shrimp with 2 mushrooms and 2 tomato wedges. Grill over low coals 2 to 3 minutes per side.
Serves 6 to 8.

Serve the tangy shrimp over cooked white rice which has been fluffed with finely chopped fresh parsley.

Fish Juan Carlos

6 to 8 fillets of fish with skin left on (or enough to weigh 3 to 4
  pounds) snapper, mackerel, trout, etc.
¾ cup lemon juice
3 teaspoons salt
1½ teaspoons paprika (Cuban, if available)
1½ teaspoons garlic salt
1½ teaspoons oregano
3 tablespoons butter

Place the fillets in a flat dish and sprinkle with half the lemon juice. Marinate for 1 hour, turning once or twice. Season the flesh side of each fillet with the salt, paprika, garlic salt, and oregano. Melt the butter in a small saucepan and add the remaining lemon juice. Place the fillets on a well-greased grill, skin side down, over low heat. Cook about 8 to 10 minutes, basting frequently with the lemon butter. Do not turn the fish.
Serves 6 to 8.

Grilled Wild Duck

1 cup soy sauce
1 cup salad oil
1½ tablespoon Liquid Smoke
salt

pepper
½ teaspoon Worcestershire sauce
¼ teaspoon dry mustard
breasts of 8 wild ducks, split and boned and skinned, making 16
   pieces

In a large bowl, combine the soy sauce, oil, Liquid Smoke, salt,
pepper, Worcestershire sauce, and mustard. Add the duck
breasts, cover, and marinate in the refrigerator overnight or at least
four hours.

Cook the breasts over moderately hot coals on a grill for 3½ to 4
minutes each side, basting constantly with reserved marinade.
They should be pink inside. Serve either whole or sliced.

Serves 6 to 8.

Mallards are best, but this is also particularly good for Florida duck.

Quail Over the Coals

16 quail
3 teaspoons paprika
½ pound butter
salt

Split the birds along the backbone with a sharp knife or poultry
shears. Flatten the birds on a firm surface to break the breastbone.
Knead the paprika into the butter and spread generously on both
sides of the bird. Cook breast down, over bright coals for 3 to 4
minutes, basting once or twice with the remaining seasoned
butter. Turn and cook 4 to 5 minutes with the bone side down,
basting with more of the seasoned butter. Dust the birds with a
little salt after removing from grill.

Serves 8.

Lamb Puccini

1 leg of lamb weighing not more than 5 pounds. Bone and
   flatten—butterfly

Sauce:

2 tablespoons prepared mustard
½ teaspoon salt
¼ teaspoon pepper
4 tablespoons brown sugar
2 tablespoons soy sauce
2 tablespoons olive oil
¼ clove garlic, crushed
⅓ cup lemon juice

Combine sauce ingredients in a small bowl. Brush lamb with mixture. Grill over medium to hot coals, turning meat several times and brushing with sauce. Check for desired degree of rareness after 30 minutes. Allow to rest before carving. Slice as you would a London broil, on the bias.
Serves 6 to 8.

Lamb Puccini may also be prepared indoors. Preheat oven to 450°, place lamb on top of rack of oven, and roast for 35 minutes, making sure to baste the meat frequently with the sauce.

Flank Steak à la Mimbo

½ cup soy sauce
½ cup salad oil
1 tablespoon Liquid Smoke
1 teaspoon bottled barbecue sauce
1 teaspoon A-1 Sauce
½ clove garlic, crushed
2 flank steaks, each weighing 2½ to 3 pounds

Mix the first 6 ingredients. Pour over flank steaks, cover, and marinate in refrigerator for several hours, turning the meat several times. Broil steaks on grill, basting several times. Cook 4 to 5 minutes on each side for rare meat. Slice against the grain in very thin slices as for London broil.
Serves 6 to 8.

This marinade may also be used for shrimp. An easy and efficient way to marinate food is in a tightly sealed plastic bag.

Steak Pizzaiola

⅓ cup cooking oil
4 garlic cloves, chopped
3 cans (28 ounces each) Italian tomatoes, undrained
salt and pepper to taste
1 pound fresh sliced mushrooms
1 small can (4 ounces) pitted ripe olives (cut in half)
5 pounds sirloin steak
3 to 4 tablespoons butter

Sauce: Heat oil over moderate heat in heavy 4-quart pot. Add garlic and sauté, being careful not to burn. Add tomatoes plus salt and pepper to taste. Break tomatoes into small pieces and cook over low heat until mixture is ⅓ original amount. Stir occasionally. Melt butter in a large, heavy skillet over moderate heat. When foam subsides, add mushrooms and sauté until light brown. Add mushrooms and olive halves to sauce. Set aside.

Grill steak over hot coals. Meat is best when rare. Transfer sauce to a large, shallow heatproof dish. Reheat sauce and add grilled steak. Cut steak into slices of desired thickness. Cutting the steak into the sauce enhances the flavor.

Serves 6 to 8.

Sauce may be made in advance and reheated while steak broils. Steak can also be prepared indoors.

Steak Roquefort

1 tender steak (3 to 4 pounds), 2 inches thick or 6 to 8 individual
  steaks
salt and pepper to taste
8 tablespoons Roquefort cheese
½ cup butter
2 to 3 tablespoons lemon juice
4 tablespoons finely chopped parsley

Broil steak to your liking. Add salt and pepper. Cream Roquefort cheese and butter with lemon juice and parsley. Serve steak immediately topped with Roquefort butter.

Serves 6 to 8.

Mr. Hector Ubertalli sets up his dining room in his studio. *Mort Kaye Studios*

Rice, Pasta, Eggs, and Cheese

Argentinian-born Hector Ubertalli is a well-known artist in the Palm Beach area, but his skills both in the kitchen and as a host rival his artistic reputation. As a single man, he is invited to many gala parties in town, and he loves to reciprocate by cooking for his friends.

His kitchen is next to his studio, but artist and chef never get together until the day of the dinner party. That morning he plans the menu and shops so that during the afternoon he will have time to do most of the cooking and write his carte du jour, taking great delight in naming some of the dishes after his guests. Since Hector the artist is very color-conscious, he takes considerable pleasure in working out the color schemes. "Warm-colored decorations make people relax," he feels, and he often uses cloths and candles in browns and sepias. At a party years ago he colored his ice cubes and now he can't stand plain ones. His guests dine in his studio among whatever canvasses and sculptures are currently taking shape.

Rice is one of his favorite dishes, and since he doesn't like to be away from his guests after their arrival, he has devised an ingenious method for cooking white rice for parties. He under-cooks the rice by half the required time, and thirty minutes before the guests arrive, adds butter to it, and places it, covered, in the top of a double boiler over medium heat. By dinnertime the rice is ready to serve al dente.

For an interesting variation of boiled white rice, he cooks one cup of rice in chicken stock, and immediately before serving adds ¼ cup mayonnaise and Parmesean cheese to taste. This is good with fried bananas.

The cuisine of Northern Italy fascinates him, and mildly seasoned lasagna made with a white sauce and generously sprinkled with freshly grated nutmeg is one of his favorite company dishes.*

*Recipe on page 175.

For brunch or lunch he loves to cook giant popovers and fill them with a crab or shrimp mixture.

Mrs. Nicholas duPont loves to be out-of-doors during the daytime hours, and she would rather be playing golf or working in the garden than spending long hours in the kitchen. Her baked rice and tomatoes* is an interesting recipe because it can be started in the morning and then finished in the oven as guests are enjoying drinks. This is good served with almost any kind of meat, but the duPonts' favorite is fried chicken.

Deviled Cheese

8 slices slightly dry bread
3 tablespoons softened butter
1 pound sharp cheddar cheese, grated
6 eggs, slightly beaten
2½ cups milk
1 small onion, grated
1½ teaspoons brown sugar
½ teaspoon salt
½ teaspoon dry mustard
½ teaspoon seasoning salt
½ teaspoon Worcestershire sauce
dash of Tabasco and pepper to taste

Preheat oven to 325°.

Spread the bread with butter. Cut 6 of the slices of bread in cubes. Take the remaining 2 slices and trim off the crusts. Cut this bread into 4 triangles. In an 8-cup buttered baking dish, make alternate layers of bread cubes and cheese. Combine all of the remaining ingredients and pour over the layers of bread and cheese. Arrange the bread triangles around the edge of the dish. Chill for several hours. About 1½ hours before serving, take from refrigerator and allow to stand at room temperature. Bake in oven for 1 hour, or until golden brown.

Serves 6 to 8.

This puffs up like a cheese soufflé. The necessity of preparing this dish ahead and refrigerating for several hours makes it an ideal item for a brunch.

*Recipe on page 173.

Eggs Carmelo

1 cup butter
1 tablespoon dried rosemary, tied in cheesecloth
8 small very ripe tomatoes, peeled and sliced thick
12 eggs
salt and pepper to taste

Melt the butter in a large, heavy skillet. Place rosemary in butter and bring to a bubble, being careful not to let the butter brown. After one minute remove the tied rosemary. Add the slices of tomato, reduce heat to medium, and cook until tomatoes are soft. Crack all eggs and put in a large bowl; season with salt and pepper. Add the unbeaten eggs all at once and mix gently. Cook mixing with a spatula only until eggs are soft scrambled.
Serves 6 to 8.

General Bradley Gaylord treasures the memory of visiting Carmelo's 3-star restaurant in Cap d'Antibes in the 1920s. The owner would present a hot ceramic dish with bubbling tomatoes and in a deft one-handed motion break the eggs into the dish, saying, "Now cook your own lunch."

Eggs à la Tripe

5 tablespoons butter
6 large onions, cut in thin slices
3 tablespoons flour
2 cups milk
1 teaspoon dry mustard
2 egg yolks
½ cup heavy cream
¼ cup grated Swiss cheese
¼ cup grated Parmesan cheese
salt
6 hot hard-boiled eggs cut in half

Preheat oven to broil.
In a large saucepan, melt 3 tablespoons of the butter over low heat. Add onions, cook covered 15 minutes until transparent and

soft but not brown. Stir occasionally. Transfer to a shallow baking dish.

Meanwhile melt remaining 2 tablespoons butter in a heavy 1½-quart saucepan. Add the flour and cook, stirring constantly over medium heat for 1 to 2 minutes. Pour in the milk, beating with a wire whisk, until well combined. Bring to a simmer and cook, stirring, until thick and smooth. Add dry mustard and salt to taste. In a small bowl beat the yolks with the cream. Stir a small amount of the hot cream sauce into the yolks and then pour back into the hot cream sauce. Stir over low heat 2 to 3 minutes. Remove from heat and stir in the Swiss cheese and half of the Parmesan cheese until melted. Adjust seasonings. Pour approximately 1 cup of the sauce over the cooked onions. Top with egg halves, cut side down. Cover evenly with rest of sauce. Sprinkle with remaining cheese. Broil until brown.

Eggs in this fashion are a favorite entrée of the Lunch Bunch

Monterey Jack Eggs

12 slices bacon, coarsely chopped
6 scallions, thinly sliced
¾ pound fresh mushrooms, sliced
12 eggs
1½ cups milk
¾ teaspoon seasoned salt
3¾ cups shredded Monterey Jack cheese

Preheat oven to 350°.

Fry bacon until browned. Drain, reserving 2 tablespoons of drippings. In large, heavy pan, sauté scallions and mushrooms in drippings until limp. Beat eggs with milk and seasoned salt. Stir in bacon, onions, mushrooms, and 3 cups of cheese. Pour mixture into a greased shallow 2-quart baking dish. Bake uncovered for 35 to 40 minutes until mixture is set and top is lightly browned. When almost done, sprinkle with remaining ¾ cup of cheese. Return to oven until cheese melts. Serve immediately.

Serves 6 to 8.

This may be prepared a day in advance up to the baking point and refrigerated. Bring to room temperature and bake as directed. It's an unusual breakfast to serve house guests.

Mushrooms Cordon Bleu

1 pound fresh mushrooms, wiped and sliced
2 cups sweet vermouth
8 slices white bread, toasted
16 slices bacon, cooked
8 slices (2 ounces each) Swiss cheese

Preheat oven broiler.
In a saucepan, boil the mushrooms in vermouth until the vermouth disappears (25 to 30 minutes). Divide mushroom mixture into 8 equal portions. Spread on top of toast. Place 2 slices of cooked bacon on top of each slice of toast. Place a slice of cheese over bacon on each sandwich. Broil until cheese is melted, watching very carefully.
Makes 8 sandwiches.

This novel sandwich would be interesting to serve after the theater, around the fire on a winter night, or for brunch.

Baked Rice, Tomatoes, and Cheese

3 tablespoons butter
⅓ cup onion, finely chopped
1 clove garlic, minced
1 cup rice, uncooked
½ cup diced tomatoes (fresh or canned)
1 sprig fresh thyme, or ¼ teaspoon dried thyme
½ bay leaf
1¼ cups chicken broth
3 to 4 tablespoons grated Parmesan cheese
3 to 4 tablespoons grated Gruyère cheese
1 tablespoon fresh parsley, chopped

Preheat oven to 400°.

Melt the butter in an ovenproof serving dish. Add onion and garlic and cook, stirring, until onion is translucent. Add rice, tomatoes, thyme, bay leaf, and broth. Stir until well mixed. Cover and bring to a boil. Remove cover. Bake in oven exactly 17 minutes. Remove from oven and take out bay leaf and thyme sprig. Stir in cheeses and parsley.
Serves 6 to 8.

Mrs. Nicholas duPont assembles this in the morning up to the point of bringing the mixture to a boil. She refrigerates it and continues the preparation just before her guests arrive.

Persian Rice

2 tablespoons butter
1⅓ cup rice, uncooked
1 cup orange juice
2 cups chicken broth
1 teaspoon salt
¾ cup raisins
¼ cup sliced toasted almonds
¼ teaspoon grated orange peel ⸜
1 tablespoon chopped parsley

In a heavy 2-quart saucepan melt the butter until hot. Add the rice and brown lightly over medium heat, stirring. Add juice, broth, salt, and raisins. Bring to a boil. Cover tightly and reduce heat to low. Cook about 25 minutes or until rice is tender. Fluff with a fork and add the almonds, orange peel, and parsley.
Serves 6 to 8.

Summer Rice

1 tablespoon butter
½ cup mushrooms, sliced very thin
3 cups cooked rice
2 cups of fresh peas, cooked
4 tablespoons chopped ripe olives
⅔ cup mayonnaise
½ cup Vinaigrette Dressing (recipe page 195)
salt and pepper

Melt butter in a small skillet over medium heat. Add mushrooms and sauté until liquid has evaporated and they are lightly browned. Remove from skillet and cool slightly. In a large serving bowl, combine the rice, peas, olives, mushrooms, and mayonnaise and the Vinaigrette Dressing. Season to taste with salt and pepper. Serve chilled.

Serves 6 to 8.

This versatile dish travels well. Take it on a picnic.

Ziti Alla Carbonara

1½ pounds bacon, diced
3 to 4 cloves garlic, minced
8 tablespoons butter
1½ pounds ziti or rigatoni noodles
6 to 8 eggs (1 per person)
⅓ cup light cream
½ cup grated Parmesan cheese

In a large skillet, cook the bacon slowly. When the bacon begins to brown, add the garlic and cook very gently. Do not let garlic brown. Drain off ½ the bacon fat and discard. Add to the bacon 8 tablespoons butter and melt. Cook ziti in rapidly boiling water according to package directions, al dente.

Meanwhile, beat eggs with the cream in a separate bowl. Put drained ziti in a large heated buttered serving bowl. Pour over the egg mixture and toss quickly to coat ziti. Pour over this the hot bacon-garlic mixture and the cheese. Toss and serve immediately.

Serves 6 to 8.

Mrs. Alva Cuddeback likes to assemble this dish at the table in a chafing dish in front of her guests, in which case she usually adapts it to serve 4 instead of 8.

Lasagna with White Sauce

breasts of 3 chickens, halved
1¼ cups of chicken broth
1 cup water
1 tablespoon salt

¼ cup cooking oil
1 pound lasagna noodles
¼ pound shredded prosciutto ham
1 cup freshly chopped parsley

Sauce:

¾ cup sweet butter
7½ tablespoons flour
2 cups milk
1½ cups whipping cream
1 cup reserved broth
½ teaspoon rosemary
½ teaspoon tarragon
½ teaspoon Beau Monde
½ teaspoon salt
dash of nutmeg
1½ cups freshly grated Parmesan cheese
chopped fresh parsley

Preheat oven to 350°.

Cook chicken breasts in a large pan with the broth and water approximately ½ hour until tender. Allow chicken to cool, then remove meat from bones. Cut chicken into bite-sized strips. Reserve broth for use in sauce. Bring at least 3 quarts of water to a rapid boil, then add 1 tablespoon salt and the cooking oil. Drop in the noodles. Cook al dente so the noodles are just a bit underdone. Drain noodles and lay to dry on a towel.

To Prepare Sauce:

In a large saucepan, melt the butter. Blend in the flour and cook, stirring constantly over medium heat for 3 minutes. Add milk, cream, and reserved broth, stirring constantly with wire whisk over low heat until mixture boils and thickens. Add seasonings. Remove from heat and stir in the cheese.

To Assemble:

Lightly butter a 9 x 13 baking dish. Place a layer of noodles on the bottom, then a layer of sauce, a layer of chicken, and shredded ham. Repeat this until the dish consists of 4 layers of noodles and sauce and 3 layers of chicken and ham. Bake 20 to 25 minutes. Before serving, top with fresh parsley.

Serves 6 to 8.

Hector Ubertalli's choice for a delicately flavored pasta.

Manicotti with Cheese Filling

Sauce:

⅓ cup olive oil
1½ cups finely chopped onion
1 clove garlic, crushed
2 cans (28 ounces each) Italian tomatoes, undrained
1 small can (6 ounces) tomato paste
2 tablespoons chopped parsley
1 tablespoon salt
1 tablespoon sugar
1 teaspoon dried oregano leaves
1 teaspoon dried basil leaves
¼ teaspoon pepper

Manicotti:

6 eggs at room temperature
1½ cups unsifted all-purpose flour
¼ teaspoon salt
1½ cups water

Filling

2 pounds ricotta cheese
½ pound mozzarella cheese, grated
⅓ cup grated Parmesan cheese
2 eggs
1 teaspoon salt

¼ teaspoon pepper
1 tablespoon chopped parsley
¼ cup grated Parmesan cheese

Preheat oven to 350°.

To Prepare Sauce:

Heat oil in a heavy 5-quart pot. Sauté the onion and garlic for 5 minutes. Mix the rest of the sauce ingredients in the pot. Bring to a boil, reduce heat, and cook covered for 1 hour. After sauce has cooled, place in a blender and turn on and off quickly 2 or 3 times. This makes the sauce very smooth.

To Prepare Manicotti:

In a medium bowl, combine eggs, flour, salt, and water. Beat until smooth with electric beater. Let stand for at least 1 hour. Heat slowly a greased omelet pan. Pour ¼ cup of batter in pan, rotating skillet quickly to spread batter evenly over bottom of pan. Cook over medium heat until batter is dry but not brown on the bottom, usually less than a minute. Flip manicotti and cook for a few seconds to set. Place on a wire rack to cool. Continue until all batter is used.

To Prepare Filling:

In a large bowl, combine all the ingredients in the order listed.

To Assemble:

Spread 1 cup of sauce in each of two 9 x 13 baking dishes. Spread each manicotti with ¼ cup of filling, roll, and place seam side down in a single layer in the dishes. Cover with remaining sauce and sprinkle with Parmesan cheese. Bake uncovered 1 hour or until bubbly.
Serves 6 to 8.

This may be completely assembled and frozen. Bring to room temperature before baking. It may also be baked in 2 layers in a single dish.

Vegetables

Mrs. Walter Gubelmann's appreciation of all things Southern belies the fact that she was born in Philadelphia. Reared in Florida, she loves okra, tomatoes, succotash, and collard greens. In fact she even raises collards and okra next to her croquet court. "They're the most expensive collard greens in Palm Beach," she says with a laugh. Grits are another of her favorites, particularly made into a soufflé.*

One of the outstanding parties that Barton Gubelmann gave was a luau on the lawn of her Palm Beach estate. She felt that a tent for weather protection would detract from the authentic feeling of the Hawaiian feast, so invitations were sent that gave an alternate rain date the following evening. Fortunately the elements cooperated, and a full moon shone through the palms just as planned. Everyone who attended remembers the spectacular centerpiece of fruits and flowers arranged on the serving table. White and green papayas, mangoes, avocados, melons, grapes, pineapples, citrus, and other tropical fruits were displayed, some cut open to expose their vivid-colored flesh and spectacular seeds. Varieties of unusual hibiscus flowers were tucked into the sprawling arrangement that stretched for five feet.

Mrs. F. Warrington Gillet, Jr., is a Southerner who also enjoys fresh produce. She frequently serves deep-fried strips of fresh squash and asparagus tips as appetizers. They are seasoned with salt and lemon juice and passed with whipped butter. She also likes to serve cold vegetables and often plans a spinach mousse† filled with seafood or marinated vegetables for warm days. Eles Gillet takes pleasure in entertaining in the beautifully refurbished

*Recipe on page 185.
†Recipe on page 196.

Tent erected and decorated for Christmas party at the home of Mr. and Mrs. F. Warrington Gillet. *Mort Kaye Studios*

Entrance to the home of Enid Haupt. *Mort Kaye Studios*

home which once belonged to her grandmother, Henrietta Ridgely Flick. She likes to give seated dinners for eighteen at her elegant long dining table. She uses place cards on place mats or a tablecloth, depending on the size of the party.

Enid Haupt is a talented horticulturist whose love for all growing things is well illustrated by the lovely gardens which are part of the Palm Beach home she designed herself. The serene, spacious rooms open onto an enclosed patio on one side and a garden on the other. As guests enter the home, they look across a low tropical garden to a shimmering mural, copied from a Monet.

Although she enjoys the company of good friends, Enid Haupt is a private person who doesn't enjoy going out so often that it becomes a chore. When she entertains, she likes to have dinner for a small group of friends, and she has emphatic ideas about the kind of food that she serves. "All the food I serve I like to be nutritious as well as appetizing. People just don't want very rich cakes and things." She cautions hostesses to remember the old rule that foods of three colors on the plate make a balanced meal. According to her observations, hers is the only house in Palm Beach or New York where bread or potatoes are still served. She believes that avoiding potatoes is a dietary wrong since a potato has no more calories than an apple and has a richer potassium content.

Her dinner menu might include a clear vegetable soup with a chicken bouillon base, boned squab roasted with wild rice and served with a fresh mushroom sauce, spiced peaches, and a salad of endive, watercress, and avocado from her garden. One of her favorite desserts is apple meringue—"a very healthy deep-dish dessert." The apples are peeled and cored, and stuffed with a mixture of raisins, walnuts, and miniature marshmallows. After they are baked and cooled, a meringue of egg whites is peaked over them and the whole dish is browned under the broiler. With it, she serves brown-edged vanilla cookies.

Black Beans José

⅓ cup olive oil
½ cup chopped onion
3 cloves garlic, crushed
1 Italian link sausage, sliced
1 teaspoon paprika
⅓ cup minced green pepper

4 cans (15 ounces each) black beans
salt and pepper

Heat olive oil in a heavy casserole. Add onion, garlic, sausage, green pepper, and paprika and cook over moderately high heat until onions are slightly browned. Add the beans, partially drained, and simmer over low heat for 1 hour. Salt and pepper to taste.
Serves 6 to 8.

This can also be baked in a 300° oven for 1 hour if desired. It is traditionally served over white rice and garnished with chopped raw onion.

Broccoli Amandine

1 large bunch broccoli (1½ pounds) or 2 packages (10 ounces each) frozen broccoli spears, cooked according to directions
4 tablespoons butter
4 tablespoons flour
1 cup cream
1 beef bouillon cube
¾ cup hot water
2 tablespoons sherry
2 tablespoons fresh lemon juice
½ teaspoon salt
½ teaspoon monosodium glutamate
¼ cup grated Parmesan cheese
¼ cup sliced toasted almonds

Preheat oven to 350°.

Clean broccoli and trim off most of the stalk. Cook in salted rapidly boiling water until just tender, about 6 minutes. Drain and place in a buttered 2-quart baking dish. Dissolve bouillon cube in ¾ cup hot water. Melt the butter in a 1-quart saucepan. Add the flour and cook over medium heat, stirring constantly, for 1 to 2 minutes. Pour in the cream and bouillon, beating vigorously with a wire whisk until combined. Cook and stir until it comes to a boil and is smooth and thickened, 3 to 5 minutes. Remove from heat and add sherry, lemon juice, salt, and monosodium glutamate.

Pour sauce over broccoli. Sprinkle with cheese and almonds. Bake uncovered for 20 minutes.

Serves 6 to 8.

Como's Cabbage

4 tablespoons butter
1 large Bermuda onion, chopped fine
2 large tart green apples, peeled, quartered, and cut into thin slices or chopped
1 cup water
1 head cabbage (2 pounds) quartered and cut into thin slices or chopped
⅓ cup light brown sugar
½ cup vinegar
salt and pepper

Melt butter in heavy 4-quart pot. Add onion and sauté over medium heat until transparent, stirring occasionally to prevent burning. Add apples, cabbage, and water. Cook covered over low heat for 1 hour, stirring occasionally. Add the sugar and vinegar, combine, and simmer 5 to 10 minutes.

Serves 6 to 8.

Mrs. Perry Como chooses this recipe because she and her husband enjoy its sweet and sour flavor.

Carrots John

1 bunch carrots (1½ pounds), cleaned, scraped, and grated
1 onion, grated, or 5 scallions, minced with green tops included
5 tablespoons butter
1 tablespoon plus 1 teaspoon flour
½ teaspoon salt
⅛ teaspoon pepper
½ cup boiling water

Sauté carrots and onion in butter, turning mixture over several times to prevent scorching. Mix in flour. Add salt and pepper and

183

½ cup boiling water and continue cooking over low heat about 20 minutes or until done.
  Serves 6 to 8.

A food processor makes the grating marvelously easy.

Corn Pudding

2 cups milk
¼ cup sugar
6 eggs, beaten well
2 tablespoons flour
2 cans (16 ounces each) creamed corn
8 tablespoons butter

  Preheat oven to 350°.
  In a mixing bowl, combine milk, sugar, eggs, and flour. Beat well with a mixer for 2 minutes. Add the creamed corn and mix well with a spoon. Pour into a shallow, buttered 13 x 9 baking dish. Dot with the butter. Bake for 45 minutes.
Allow it to set a few minutes before serving.
  Serves 6 to 8.

Eggplant Soufflé

1 medium eggplant, peeled and sliced
2 tablespoons butter
2 tablespoons flour
1 cup milk
1 cup grated Parmesan cheese
1 teaspoon salt
1 teaspoon pepper
3 egg yolks
3 egg whites

  Preheat oven to 350°.
  Grease and flour a 2-quart soufflé dish. Cook eggplant slices in a small amount of boiling water until tender, about 10 minutes. Drain them well and mash them.
  In a 1½-quart saucepan melt the butter. Add the flour and cook over medium heat, stirring constantly for 1 to 2 minutes. Pour in

the milk, beating vigorously with a wire whisk until combined. Bring to a boil and cook, stirring until smooth and thick. Remove from heat and add cheese and salt and pepper. Cool 5 minutes at room temperature. Add egg yolks and blend well. Slowly stir in mashed eggplant. Beat egg whites until stiff but not dry and fold gently into eggplant mixture. Pour into soufflé dish and bake 30 to 45 minutes until golden and puffed.

Serves 6 to 8.

Hominy Grits Soufflé

¾ cup uncooked hominy grits
1 cup boiling water
2 cups milk
4 tablespoons melted butter
4 egg yolks, well beaten
salt
white pepper
6 egg whites

Preheat oven to 350°.

Grease a 2½-quart soufflé dish and dust with flour. Pour the rapidly boiling water into a 1½-quart saucepan and pour in the grits. Cook over medium heat for 2 minutes, stirring constantly. Stir in 1 cup of the milk and set the saucepan over boiling water. Cook for 30 minutes. Remove from heat and stir in the remaining cup of milk and the melted butter. Place this again over boiling water and stir until the mixture is smooth and heated through. Add salt and pepper to taste. Remove from the fire and stir in the well-beaten egg yolks. Cool to lukewarm.

Meanwhile, in a large bowl beat the egg whites until stiff but not dry. Fold the whites into the hominy mixture. Pour into the prepared dish and bake 45 minutes.

Serves 6 to 8.

Mrs. Walter Gubelmann serves this Southern favorite at her wild game dinners.

Delmonico Potatoes

9 medium-sized red potatoes, boiled until nearly done
½ pound sharp cheddar cheese, grated
1 teaspoon dry mustard
1½ teaspoons salt
1 cup heavy cream
1 cup milk
dash pepper
pinch of nutmeg

Preheat oven to 325°.
Peel and grate potatoes and place in a buttered 1½-quart casserole. In a 1-quart saucepan combine cheese, mustard, salt, and pepper, nutmeg, cream, and milk. Stir over low heat until cheese melts. Pour over potatoes. Do not stir. Bake uncovered 45 to 60 minutes.
Serves 6 to 8.

This can be assembled in advance and refrigerated, covered. Bring to room temperature and bake as above.

Potatoes Italian

4 large baking potatoes
1 tablespoon olive oil
3 medium tomatoes, sliced
1 large Spanish onion, peeled and thinly sliced
¼ cup grated Parmesan cheese
1 cup shredded provolone cheese
½ cup shredded mozzarella cheese
½ teaspoon oregano
1½ teaspoons salt
⅛ teaspoon pepper
2 tablespoons butter

Preheat oven to 400°.
Peel and slice potatoes ¼ inch thick. Oil a large 9 x 13 casserole dish with the olive oil. Combine the three cheeses. Arrange

potatoes, tomatoes, and onion slices in layers, sprinkling each layer with cheeses and seasonings, ending with a layer of potatoes sprinkled with the cheeses and seasonings. Dot with butter and bake uncovered 50 minutes or until vegetables are tender and the top is crusty brown.

Serves 6 to 8.

Ratatouille

2 medium eggplants, peeled and sliced ½ inch thick
2 zucchini, sliced ½ inch thick
1 cup olive oil
salt and pepper
3 cups chopped onion
2 cloves garlic, crushed
2 red or green peppers, seeded and cut into strips
1 pound ripe tomatoes, peeled and chopped
2 tablespoons freshly chopped parsley
1 cup crushed potato chips
¼ cup grated Parmesan cheese

Preheat oven to 325°.

Sprinkle the eggplants and zucchini slices liberally with salt on both sides and set in a colander or on paper towels for 1 hour to allow moisture to escape. Dry well with paper towels. Pour in enough oil to cover the bottom of a large, heavy skillet. Place over moderately high heat. When a haze forms, add enough eggplant slices to comfortably fit in pan, and brown on both sides. Transfer the browned slices to a large, deep, buttered 5-quart casserole. Sprinkle with salt and pepper. Proceed with the rest of the eggplant, using more oil as needed. In the same skillet sauté the zucchini in the same manner, adding more oil as necessary and spread in a layer over eggplant. Then sauté onion and garlic and spread over zucchini. Salt and pepper each layer. Make another layer of the raw green pepper and then the raw tomatoes, seasoning each. Sprinkle with parsley. Top with the crushed chips and cheese and bake for 45 minutes.

Serves 6 to 8.

Ratatouille may be made a day in advance, brought to room temperature, and baked as directed. Can be served warm or cold.

Sautéed Scallions

2 tablespoons butter
3 bunches scallions (approximately 36) trimmed to 5 inches
salt and pepper

Melt butter in a large, heavy skillet over medium heat. Add scallions and sauté over moderately high heat for 3 minutes. Cover and turn heat to very low, then simmer for 5 more minutes.
Serves 6 to 8.

Baked Cucumbers

6 cucumbers, peeled, seeded and cut into 2-inch strips ½ inch wide
2 tablespoons wine vinegar
½ teaspoon salt
⅛ teaspoon sugar
3 tablespoons butter, melted
½ teaspoon basil or dill
3 to 4 tablespoon minced scallions, green tops included
⅛ teaspoon pepper

Preheat oven to 375 degrees.
Soak the cucumber pieces in the vinegar, salt and sugar for 30 minutes, tossing a few times to coat. Drain on paper towels and pat dry. In a shallow 12 x 8 baking dish stir the melted butter, basil or dill, scallions and pepper. Add the cucumber, toss to coat, and bake uncovered 1 hour or until tender. Toss once or twice while baking. Garnish with chopped parsley if desired.
Serves 6 to 8.

Italian Spinach Pie

1 9-inch pastry shell
1½ cups cooked and chopped fresh spinach, or 2 boxes (10 ounces each) frozen chopped spinach, cooked
4 tablespoons butter
salt and freshly ground pepper
½ pound ricotta cheese

½ cup freshly grated Parmesan cheese
3 eggs, slightly beaten
½ cup heavy cream
grated nutmeg

Preheat oven to 450°.

Chill pie shell. Prick bottom with fork and bake for 10 to 15 minutes, being sure not to brown crust. Cool. Reset oven to 375°. Drain and squeeze the cooked chopped spinach. Stir in butter, salt, and pepper to taste. In a large mixing bowl place the ricotta and Parmesan cheese, eggs, cream, and nutmeg. Beat with an electric mixer 2 to 3 minutes. Stir in the cooked spinach and combine well. Pour into baked shell and bake 30 minutes.

Serves 6 to 8.

The pastry and filling may be prepared early in the day and refrigerated separately. Remove filling from refrigerator 1 hour before assembling.

Squash Gratiné

1½ pounds fresh yellow squash, cut up
⅔ cup chopped onion
2 eggs, well beaten
3 slices bacon, cooked and crumbled
1 cup grated cheddar cheese
4 saltine crackers, crushed
salt and pepper
2 tablespoons butter
¼ cup grated Parmesan cheese

Preheat oven to 350°.

Cook squash and onion in a small amount of water in a covered pan until just tender, 6 to 8 minutes. Drain well and mash with a fork. Combine with eggs, bacon, cheese, saltines, and salt and pepper. Pour into a greased 2-quart buttered baking dish. Dot with butter and sprinkle with Parmesan. Bake 30 to 40 minutes.

Serves 6 to 8.

Tomatoes Florentine

2 packages (10 ounces each) frozen chopped spinach
4½ tablespoons butter
¼ cup minced scallions
¼ cup dry bread crumbs
2 eggs slightly beaten
¼ cup freshly grated Parmesan cheese
½ teaspoon minced garlic
¼ teaspoon thyme
¼ teaspoon salt
⅛ teaspoon fresh pepper
8 large thick tomato slices (about ½ inch thick)
½ teaspoon garlic salt

Preheat oven to 350°.

Cook spinach according to package directions and drain well. In a small skillet, melt ½ tablespoon of the butter and add scallions. Sauté until soft. Combine the spinach with the bread crumbs, sautéed scallions, eggs, Parmesan cheese, garlic, remaining butter, thyme, salt, and pepper. Arrange tomato slices in shallow buttered baking dish. Sprinkle with garlic salt. Spoon ¼ cup of the spinach mixture on each tomato slice and shape it into a dome. Bake 15 to 20 minutes or until heated through.

Serves 6 to 8.

Fanned Zucchini

6 to 8 zucchini (approximately 2 pounds)
¼ cup olive oil
2 tablespoons butter
⅓ cup freshly grated Parmesan cheese
salt and freshly ground pepper

Preheat oven to 400°.

Plunge whole zucchini into a large saucepan of salted boiling water; when water returns to a boil, cover and boil slowly 10 to 12 minutes. Remove zucchini and allow to cool. Leaving the stem end intact, make 3 or 4 slices in each zucchini lengthwise to the stem. Fan slices and place in a gratin dish in a single layer. Drizzle oil over zucchini. Dot with butter. Sprinkle with the cheese, salt, and pepper. Bake 10 to 15 minutes or until brown.

Serves 6 to 8.

The dining room of the home of Mr. and Mrs. Robert Gardiner. *Mort Kaye Studios*

Salads

Mrs. H. Loy Anderson enjoys unplanned informal entertaining, and on any Sunday morning she's prepared to feed from four to fourteen when her grown children and their friends drop in for pancakes and sausage. Louisiana-born Thérèse Anderson employs a cook from Nassau, and the two combine their talents to plan menus that feature both Creole and Bahamian dishes like jambalaya, peas and rice, and shrimp Creole. Lunch is a great way "to gather up friends" Anderson-style, and Louisiana Shrimp Salad* is a popular choice for a sultry Florida summer day. During the winter Mrs. Anderson adds a hot gumbo to the salad menu, but in any season of the year she likes warm pecan pie for dessert.

Lunch is also get-together time for the Lunch Bunch, a group of eight who started meeting once a week three years ago and still have a steady Monday date. Mrs. Bedford Davie began the tradition by asking seven friends (Mrs. William T. Young, Mrs. Iva Patcevitch, Mrs. Thomas Shevlin, Mrs. M. H. McLean, Mrs. Charles Amory, Mrs. Alberto Farinas, and Mrs. Elena Echarte) to join her for lunch. Even though five of the members work (they are dubbed the "merchants" while the other three are known as the "swells"), each takes turn entertaining the others at her home on Mondays. No other guests are invited and membership is limited to the original eight. Even a dress code is prescribed. The merchants wear navy blue while the swells must dress in pastel colors.

Competition is fierce as one hostess outdoes the other in presenting a fabulous lunch. Menus run the gamut from Durie Shevlin's beef curry with all the condiments or her delicious bouillabaisse to Chessy Patcevitch's Eggs à la Tripe,* salad, and

*Recipe on page 171.

soufflé. Another of Mrs. Patcevitch's favorites is cold lump crabmeat lightly laced with homemade mayonnaise and garnished with melon wedges. With this she serves a green salad and a slice of fresh pineapple topped with pineapple ice cream. Dysie Davie likes baby pompano and a mixed green salad of Brussels sprouts, green beans, and lima beans served with a tart French dressing. Dessert might be warmed Kadota figs with sour cream or a scoop of fruit ice frozen with a surprise core of an appropriate liqueur or dark rum.

Mrs. Robert Gardiner is a one-time vegetarian and still an avid health enthusiast, who always eats a fresh vegetable salad for lunch at home. Although two Chinese cooks reign over her kitchen, Mrs. Gardiner fixes her own luncheon salads combining Bibb lettuce, fresh bean and alfalfa sprouts, fresh mushrooms, cucumber, avocado, raw spinach, and raw crookneck squash seasoned with garden-fresh basil. She uses no other seasonings, oil, or dressing, but supplements the salad with a slice of seven-grain bread from a health food store. On a kitchen windowsill she raises sprouts of mung beans and alfalfa, which grow green in the sunshine. The Chinese cooks show their disapproval of her gardening technique by growing their own white sprouts away from the light.

In their formal dining room overlooking a secluded arm of Lake Worth and an island bird sanctuary, the Gardiners often seat fourteen for an authentic Chinese dinner. Cocktails accompanied with a pâté or caviar precede a multicourse meal of egg drop soup, rice, chicken breasts stuffed with water chestnuts, thinly sliced filet of beef with Chinese baked noodles and mung bean sprouts, shrimp with vegetables, and salad of bean sprouts and snow peas. Fresh Chinese fruits such as lychee nuts are passed for dessert. The long Chippendale table, made in the eighteenth century for Robert Gardiner's ancestors, .is set with exquisite French linen, formal silver, and wooden chopsticks.

Asparagus and Avocado Salad

2 bunches fresh asparagus (approximately 2 pounds)
1 avocado (not too ripe)
½ cup Vinaigrette Dressing
6 to 8 radishes

lettuce leaves
2 teaspoons finely chopped parsley

Scrape the asparagus stalks with a vegetable peeler and cut off the tough ends. Cut off the tips and set aside. Cut the stalks on the bias into 1-inch pieces. Bring a saucepan of salted water to a boil. Place the tips in water for 2 minutes of boiling time. Remove and drain. Add the stalks for 4 minutes of boiling time. Remove and drain. Peel the avocado, cut into 2-inch cubes, and place in a salad bowl. Pour over the Vinaigrette Dressing immediately to prevent discoloration. Trim the radishes, slice very thinly, and cut into julienne strips. Add to avocado. Add the cooled asparagus pieces and toss lightly. Serve on a bed of lettuce and sprinkle with parsley.
Serves 6 to 8.

Vinaigrette Dressing:

2 tablespoons red wine vinegar
6 tablespoons olive oil
1 teaspoon prepared Dijon-style mustard
1 teaspoon lemon juice
½ teaspoon sugar
1 teaspoon salt
pepper to taste

Combine all ingredients in a screwtop jar and mix well.

Avocado and Grapefruit Salad

3 to 4 medium avocados cut in half lengthwise with meat carefully removed, leaving skin-shell intact
3 to 4 grapefruit, peeled, seeded, and sectioned
1 head Boston, Bibb or iceburg lettuce, cleaned
dressing

Slice avocado meat and combine with grapefruit sections. Divide them equally among the empty avocado shells, which will be used as "bowls." Combine all dressing ingredients in a bowl or screwtop jar and mix well. Arrange salad on lettuce leaves and pour dressing over each serving.
Serves 6 to 8.

Dressing

2 cups salad oil
½ cup vinegar
6 tablespoons sugar
1 small onion, grated
¼ cup sour cream
pinch of salt and pepper

Cold Spinach Mousse

2 tablespoons peanut or vegetable oil
3 packages (10 ounces each) frozen chopped spinach
1 teaspoon salt
½ teaspoon freshly grated black pepper
½ teaspoon freshly grated nutmeg
1 small yellow onion, peeled and grated
1 cup mayonnaise
2 tablespoons unflavored gelatin
1 tablespoon lemon juice
1 cup heavy cream
green mayonnaise

Brush a 6-cup ring mold with oil; turn upside down on paper towels to drain off excess. Set the mold aside. Cook spinach according to package directions. Drain well and squeeze out all excess moisture. Chop very fine. Place in large bowl, season with salt, pepper, and nutmeg and stir in grated onion and mayonnaise. Sprinkle gelatin over the lemon juice to soften. Set in a pan of hot water and stir until dissolved. Whip the cream until it holds a shape. Fold in the gelatin mixture, fold cream into spinach mixture, and pour into the prepared mold. Chill 2 hours. To serve, unmold and dress with green mayonnaise.
Serves 6 to 8.

Green Mayonnaise

12 watercress leaves
6 sprigs parsley
13 spinach leaves
2 cups mayonnaise

Drop the watercress leaves, parsley sprigs, and spinach leaves into boiling water. Blanch for 1 minute. Drain and refresh in cold water. Drain well, squeeze dry, and mince. Stir into mayonnaise.

Mrs. F. Warrington Gillet, Jr., fills the center with a cold seafood salad or Vegetables Vinaigrette (recipe page 203).

Caesar Salad

2 teaspoons salt
1 teaspoon pepper
2 cloves garlic, crushed
1 teaspoon anchovy paste
¼ teaspoon dry mustard
¼ teaspoon Worcestershire sauce
5 tablespoons Parmesan cheese
2 tablespoons wine vinegar
2 tablespoons lemon juice
½ cup olive oil
2 raw egg yolks
1 large head of Romaine lettuce, cleaned and torn into large pieces
½ cup croutons

In a large wooden salad bowl, place the salt, pepper, and garlic. Mash ingredients against the side of the bowl with a wooden spoon. Add the anchovy paste and mash again. Add the mustard, Worcestershire sauce, and one tablespoon of the cheese, mixing well. With a fork beat in the vinegar, lemon juice, and oil. Beat in the egg yolks. Add Romaine pieces to the bowl and toss well. Sprinkle with four tablespoons Parmesan and the croutons. Serves 6 to 8.

Guava Shells with Cottage Cheese and Lemon Dressing

2 cans (15½ ounces each) guava shells
1 pint cottage cheese
1 head Bibb lettuce, washed and dried
lemon dressing

Drain guava shells. Fill with a scoop of cottage cheese. Arrange on a bed of lettuce on a large platter or on individual plates. Serve with lemon dressing.

Lemon Dressing

1 cup fresh lemon juice, strained
2 cups soya oil
½ cup sugar
½ teaspoon salt

Place all ingredients in a screwtop jar and shake well. Serves 6 to 8.

The drained guava shells may be served with cream cheese and crackers as a dessert.

Land and Sea Salad

6 cups torn salad greens
1 ripe tomato, cut into chunks
2 eggs, hard-boiled and sliced
½ ripe avocado, sliced
1 cup shredded Monterey Jack cheese
5 radishes, sliced
1 can (6½ ounces) tuna fish, drained
½ pound sliced bacon, chopped, cooked, and drained.
Buttermilk Salad Dressing

In a large bowl, combine all the ingredients except the dressing. Do not season. Pass the Buttermilk Salad Dressing separately. Serves 6 to 8.

By adding rolls and fruit to the menu this salad becomes a main dish for a light summer supper.

Buttermilk Salad Dressing

1⅓ cups mayonnaise
1 cup plus 1 tablespoon buttermilk

1 teaspoon garlic salt
1 teaspoon monosodium glutamate
⅓ teaspoon salt
1 teaspoon pepper
2 tablespoons chopped fresh parsley

In a bowl or a screwtop jar, blend all ingredients well.

Ports of Call Salad

1 large head Romaine lettuce, washed, dried, and torn in pieces
½ pound yellow squash in julienne strips
4 tablespoons chopped fresh parsley
Ports of Call Salad Dressing

Mix salad greens and vegetables in a large salad bowl and toss with just enough dressing to lightly coat leaves.

Ports of Call Salad Dressing

3 egg yolks
½ teaspoon dry mustard
½ cup peanut oil
1 cup mayonnaise
¼ cup buttermilk
1 tablespoon lemon juice
¼ teaspoon Tabasco
1½ teaspoons Worcestershire sauce
1 ounce anchovy fillets, minced
½ clove garlic, crushed
2 tablespoons Parmesan cheese
2 tablespoons white vinegar
salt and pepper to taste

Mix yolks and mustard. Gradually beat in oil until thick. Add mayonnaise and buttermilk blending until smooth. Add all of the remaining ingredients while beating constantly.
Serves 6 to 8.

Salad Romano

½ pound Gruyère or Swiss cheese, sliced very thin and cut into
   julienne strips, 1½ inches long
8 medium mushrooms, wiped clean and sliced very thin
6 ribs of celery, sliced very thin on the bias
2 tablespoons of chopped fresh parsley
Vinaigrette Dressing (recipe page 195)
6 to 8 lettuce leaves

   Combine the above ingredients in a salad bowl with the dressing
and toss lightly. Allow to stand 15 to 20 minutes before serving.
Serve on lettuce leaves.
   Serves 6 to 8.

Try as a first course when the menu does not include another salad.

Artichokes Stuffed with Shrimp Salad

2 tablespoons olive oil
1½ tablespoons salt per quart of water
6 to 8 artichokes
4 pounds shrimp, cooked, shelled, and chilled
4 small shallots or scallions, minced
4 tablespoons whole capers
1 clove of garlic, crushed
¾ cup chopped fresh parsley
salt and pepper
Tarragon Dressing

   Bring to a boil about 7 quarts of water to which the oil and salt
have been added. Cut the stems from the artichokes. Pull off the
tough bottom row of leaves and cut off ¼ of the tops of the leaves
with scissors. Add the artichokes to the boiling water. Cover and
boil about 40 minutes. Drain. When cool enough to handle,
carefully remove the choke in the middle of the vegetable by
pulling through the top with the help of a spoon. Cut shrimp into
bite-sized pieces and place in a large bowl. Add shallots, capers,
garlic, parsley, and salt and pepper and combine. Pour the

dressing over the shrimp. Adjust seasoning. Mix well. Fill artichoke cavity with shrimp

Serves 6 to 8.

This makes a pretty luncheon dish. Make a double portion of dressing to serve in small bowls for dipping the artichoke leaves.

Tarragon Dressing

¾ cup olive oil
4 tablespoons wine vinegar
½ teaspoon dry mustard
2 tablespoons lemon juice
1 teaspoon freshly ground pepper
2 teaspoons tarragon

Combine all ingredients in a screwtop jar or bowl and mix well.

Louisiana Shrimp Salad

2 tablespoons vinegar
4 tablespoons olive oil
1 tablespoon prepared mustard
2 scallions with tops, minced
2 stalks celery, minced
½ tablespoon lime juice
1 clove garlic, minced
salt and pepper to taste
1 hard-boiled egg, chopped
3 pounds shelled, deveined, and cooked shrimp
6 to 8 tomato slices
1 head lettuce, washed and crisped

In a bowl, mix the dressing ingredients in the order listed. Add cooked shrimp, tossing well with dressing. Refrigerate for at least 2 hours. When ready to serve, mix again. Arrange each portion on a slice of tomato in a bed of lettuce.

Serves 6 to 8.

A favorite of Mrs. H. Loy Anderson, who grew up enjoying shellfish from the Gulf.

Roast Beef Salad

5 cups cooked roast beef (approximately 2 pounds), cut into
  julienne strips
1 medium green pepper, thinly sliced
1 medium onion, thinly sliced
1½ cups sliced fresh mushrooms
2 cups sliced celery
lettuce leaves
Ports of Call Salad Dressing (recipe page 199), substituting 2 to 3
  tablespoons crumbled blue cheese for the Parmesan cheese

In a large mixing bowl, mix together the roast beef strips, green
pepper, onion, mushrooms, and celery. Chill. Just before serving
toss with Ports of Call dressing. Serve on individual beds of
lettuce.
Serves 6 to 8.

Spinach Salad

⅔ cup salad oil
¼ cup red wine vinegar
1 clove garlic, crushed
2 teaspoons soy sauce
1 teaspoon sugar
1 teaspoon dry mustard
½ teaspoon curry powder
½ teaspoon salt
½ teaspoon freshly ground pepper
2 bunches fresh spinach, washed, dried, and torn as for a salad
8 slices bacon, cooked, then crumbled
4 eggs, hard-boiled and chopped fine

Mix well in a small bowl the oil, vinegar, garlic, soy sauce, sugar,
mustard, curry powder, salt, and pepper. Place spinach in a large
salad bowl. Pour dressing over. Add bacon and eggs and toss well.
Serves 6 to 8.

Curried Turkey Salad

½ cup mayonnaise
½ cup plain yogurt
¼ cup dairy sour cream
2 tablespoons lemon juice
2 teaspoons curry powder
1½ teaspoons onion salt
4 cups diced cooked turkey
½ cup chopped celery
1 cup chopped fresh pineapple (if unavailable substitute 1 cup
  chopped apple)
1 head Boston lettuce, washed and dried
1 bunch watercress, washed and dried

Mix together in a large bowl all ingredients except lettuce and watercress. Arrange lettuce and watercress in large serving bowl or on individual plates and place a mound of the turkey salad in center of each.
Serves 6 to 8.

Vegetables Vinaigrette

1 pound fresh green beans, cleaned
4 carrots, scraped and sliced thinly on the bias
3 stalks celery, sliced thinly on the bias
½ small head of cauliflower, broken into flowerets
¼ pound mushrooms, sliced very thin
3 tablespoons freshly chopped parsley
lettuce leaves
Vinaigrette Dressing (recipe page 195)

Bring 1 quart of water to a boil over high heat. Add 1 tablespoon salt. Add beans and boil for only 5 minutes. Remove to a large bowl with a slotted spoon. Add carrots and celery to same boiling water and cook only 2 minutes. Remove with a slotted spoon to the bowl with beans. Add the cauliflower to the same water and boil for 4 minutes. Remove with slotted spoon and add to other crisp cooked vegetables. Combine drained vegetables, mushrooms, and parsley and toss well with the Vinaigrette Dressing. Chill slightly and serve on a lettuce leaf.
Serves 6 to 8.

Watercress Salad

8 tablespoons olive oil
2 tablespoons wine vinegar
1 tablespoon lemon juice
1 tablespoon curry powder
salt and pepper
6 bunches watercress, washed, dried, and chilled in a damp towel
3 oranges, peeled and sectioned
2 teaspoons finely chopped shallots

In a small bowl or jar, combine oil, vinegar, lemon juice, curry powder, salt, and pepper. Mix well. Place the watercress in a salad bowl. Add the orange sections and shallots. Pour in the dressing and toss.
Serves 6 to 8.

Zucchini with Sauce Tartare

1 small zucchini per person, unpeeled, coarsely grated into a bowl

Sauce Tartare

2 hard-boiled eggs
2 raw egg yolks
1 tablespoon Dijon-style mustard
¼ teaspoon salt
1 cup oil
3 to 4 tablespoons minced capers
3 tablespoons minced dill pickle
2 to 4 tablespoons minced parsley, chives, or tarragon
1 to 2 tablespoons lemon juice

Sieve yolks of hard-boiled eggs. Chop white coarsely. In a bowl, mix sieved and raw yolks with mustard and salt. Use an electric beater at low spead. Add the oil drop by drop. When it is obviously being absorbed and the mixture becomes creamy, dribble in the remainder of the oil slowly while continuing to beat. When all the oil has been added, stir in the capers, pickle, and herbs. Add lemon juice to taste. Lastly add the chopped egg whites and mix. Pour the sauce into the bowl with the grated zucchini. Stir until well combined. Cover and refrigerate. Serve on a bed of lettuce if desired.
Serves 6 to 8.

Mushroom Salad

1 pound new potatoes
1 pound mushrooms, cleaned and sliced thin
1 tablespoon chervil
½ teaspoon salt
⅛ teaspoon dry mustard
⅓ cup tarragon vinegar
⅓ cup olive oil
3 tablespoons freshly chopped parsley

Drop the new potatoes into a saucepan with enough boiling water to cover them. Cover the pan and cook until tender, about 20 to 30 minutes. Cool, remove the skins, and slice thinly. In a bowl combine the cooled potato slices with the mushrooms, chervil, salt, mustard, vinegar, and oil. Stir gently until well mixed. Chill in refrigerator. Before serving, sprinkle with the parsley and toss lightly. May be served chilled or at room temperature.
Serves 6 to 8.

This would be an interesting addition to an antipasto.

Herbed Tomatoes

6 to 8 ripe tomatoes peeled and thickly sliced
⅔ cup olive oil
1 cup vinegar
¼ cup chopped scallions, including some of the green tops
¼ cup freshly chopped parsley
1 teaspoon salt
¼ teaspoon ground pepper
2 teaspoons thyme
1 clove garlic, crushed
3 tablespoons sugar

Place sliced tomatoes in a large flat serving dish. Mix the remaining ingredients together and pour over tomatoes. Cover and refrigerate for at least 6 hours.
Serves 6 to 8.

Mrs. William T. Young, Jr., in the kitchen of her Palm Beach home with her children.

Desserts

A sweet is usually thought of as the impressive finale of a well-rounded meal, but it can also be savored with tea in the afternoon to boost flagging energy and drooping spirits.

One Palm Beach hostess who delights in the ceremony of afternoon tea is Mrs. Wiley Reynolds. "Tea is fun," she believes, and following afternoon meetings she invites a small group of friends to join her for tea in her lovely Tarpon Island home. As daylight wanes, they sit around the table in the candlelit dining room and enjoy a bracing pot of tea, a comforting array of confections, and good conversation.

Mrs. Reynolds changes the type of tea she serves with the changing seasons, prefering orange pekoe and Ceylon varieties. Her four components for tea-table fare are sandwiches, fruit, something hot, and a sweet. Watercress and ham are her favorite tea sandwiches; strawberries, slices of apple, dried figs, and dates grace the fruit plate. Chocolate-dipped Australian apricots from a gourmet counter are sometimes added. Something hot might be crisp toast or English muffins with ginger marmalade. For the sweet, Janet Reynolds serves a chocolate cake which is justifiably famous. The recipe has been cherished since her mother-in-law's cake made its public debut at Bethesda Church Lenten teas during the thirties.

Mrs. William T. Young, Jr., includes dessert in all her party menus, and one of her favorites is one that guests can drink with a straw. Heavenlies* combine ice cream and liqueur in a smooth portable dessert which guests can sip while relaxing in the living room or loggia after dinner.

Franci Young loves to entertain in the casual open house her husband christened the Villa Vanilla. Organization is her key to

*Recipe on page 209.

207

successful entertaining, and she uses her energy most efficiently as she divides her time between her home and her studio. A long guest list doesn't faze her a bit. "I think I should cook in a logging camp because I can't cook for only three," she moans. She does her own cooking before a party and then relies on extra help for serving so that she can enjoy the role of hostess.

A party with a theme or in honor of a special occasion is her métier. Humorous handwritten invitations, composed by General Young, set the tone, and her careful attention to the smallest detail adds a unique touch to the affair. Mrs. Young's lucky guests have sometimes found a piece of her well-known porcelain individualized as a place card. One Easter Sunday when the patio was transformed into a Marseilles café, each place was marked with a bouillabaisse bowl handpainted with a guest's name. At another party with an Austrian theme, a large porcelain pig crowned with sausages presided over the buffet table, and a gaily painted wheelbarrow held beer and champagne in ice on the patio.

Some Palm Beachers prefer to serve a simple fruit dessert and follow it with a coffee specialty—perhaps a highly spiced coffee or a strong Cuban variety with spoonfuls of multicolored sugar crystals, or a caffè granito, a shaved ice of espresso topped with sweetened cream. The large citrus groves and strawberry farms in the area provide luscious fruit for the inventive hostess to use, and many Florida gardens have bananas, key limes, and coconuts for easy harvesting. Whether the meal is brought to a close with a masterpiece of cream and calories or a compote of refreshing fruit, Palm Beach guests look forward to dessert.

Cold Chocolate Cream

2 packages (4 ounces each) ladyfingers
2 packages (4 ounces each) German chocolate
2 tablespoons hot coffee
4 egg yolks
2 teaspoons confectioner's sugar
1 teaspoon vanilla
4 egg whites
2 cups heavy cream
2 teaspoons sugar

Line a 9 x 5 x 2 loaf pan with foil. Place split ladyfingers around sides and bottom of pan. In a double boiler, over hot water melt the chocolate with the hot coffee. Beat in egg yolks one at a time. Add sugar and vanilla, mixing well. In a separate bowl, beat the egg whites until stiff but not dry and fold gently into the chocolate mixture. Pour into lined pan. Refrigerate for 24 hours.

Remove from refrigerator and unmold onto serving plate. Whip cream, blending in the 2 teaspoons sugar. Frost the mold completely with the whipped cream. Shaved chocolate may be added for decoration.

Serves 6 to 8.

Heavenlies

2 quarts coffee or vanilla ice cream, softened
½ cup rum or brandy

Place ice cream in blender. Add rum or brandy and blend to the consistency of a thick milk shake. Pour into stem glasses and serve with a straw.

Serves 6 to 8.

This may be prepared in advance and frozen in the blender container. Before serving blend about 30 seconds at high speed. Franci Young varies her Heavenlies with different flavors of ice cream, sherbet, and liqueur.

Chocolate Almond Soufflé

3 egg yolks
½ cup sugar
2 teaspoons almond extract
4 ounces unsweetened chocolate, melted in a double boiler over
    hot water
4 egg whites
pinch salt
⅛ teaspoon cream of tartar

Preheat oven to 400°.

Butter a 4-cup soufflé dish and dust with confectioner's sugar. Beat the egg yolks in a mixing bowl. Add the sugar and continue to beat until light in color. Stir in the almond extract. Fold in melted chocolate and cool slightly. In a separate bowl beat egg whites with salt and cream of tartar until stiff. Gently fold the chocolate mixture into the egg whites. Pour into prepared soufflé dish. Place in oven and reduce temperature to 375°. Bake 15 to 20 minutes.

Serves 6 to 8.

Blueberries and Banana Cream

4 cups fresh blueberries, cleaned
1 cup heavy cream
¼ cup sugar
2 ripe bananas, peeled
¾ teaspoon grated lemon rind

Divide blueberries in 6 to 8 sherbet glasses or bowls. In a bowl whip the cream with sugar until it begins to thicken. In a separate bowl mash the bananas with a fork until smooth. Add lemon rind. Combine the mashed bananas and lemon rind with the cream mixture. Whip until blended and thickened but still soft enough to pour. Pour over berries and serve.

Serves 6 to 8.

Masked Figs

12 to 16 dried figs
¾ cup finely minced, blanched, toasted almonds
2 tablespoons honey
¾ cup ruby port
1 cup heavy cream, whipped and sweetened

Preheat oven to 250°.

Steam dried figs for 5 to 10 minutes until plump. (To steam figs place in a strainer in saucepan with enough water to boil but not to touch the figs. Cover and steam.) Remove and slice a pocket in the side of each fig. Combine the almonds with the honey and place a large teaspoonful of mixture into each pocket. Reshape neatly. Place the stuffed figs in a shallow baking dish just large enough to hold them. Pour in the port. Place in refrigerator overnight or let stand at room temperature for 2 to 3 hours. Bake 20 to 25 minutes. Top each serving with whipped cream.

Serves 6 to 8.

Strawberries on Ice

½ cup sour cream
¼ cup heavy cream, whipped
4 tablespoons brown sugar
2 tablespoons Grand Marnier liqueur
¼ cup Curaçao liqueur
1 tablespoon dark Myers rum
crushed ice
3 pints fresh strawberries, cleaned with stems still attached

In a small bowl, combine the sour cream, whipped cream, and sugar. Stir in the Grand Marnier, Curaçao, and rum. Mix well and transfer to a small serving dish.
Serves 6 to 8.

In a large, deep serving platter mound crushed ice, leaving an indentation in the center for the bowl of dipping sauce. Set the strawberries around the sauce, directly on the ice.

Galliano Compote

1 cup red currant jelly
2 tablespoons orange juice
¼ cup Galliano liqueur
1 grapefruit, peeled and sliced or sectioned
1 orange, peeled and sliced or sectioned
1 bunch grapes, halved and seeded
1 apple, cored and sliced

In a small saucepan, melt jelly over low heat. Stir in orange juice and liqueur. Cool. Serve over fruit that has been placed in a serving bowl.
Serves 6 to 8.

Sun Ray Compote

1 cup watermelon balls
8 slices cantaloupe
8 slices Cranshaw melon
8 grapefruit, peeled and sectioned
16 orange sections

Mound watermelon balls in center of serving platter. Arrange the remaining fruit around the center like rays of sun. Serve with Banana Dressing.
Serves 6 to 8.

Banana Dressing

2 ripe bananas
2 tablespoons lemon juice
¼ cup brown sugar
¼ cup honey
1 cup heavy cream, whipped

Using a blender, combine bananas, lemon juice, sugar, and honey until smooth. Fold into whipped cream.

This was a specialty of Mar-a-Lago. Mrs. Marjorie Merriweather Post often served it as a salad.

Bananas Tropicale

6 slightly green bananas, peeled and split lengthwise
3 tablespoons butter, melted
⅓ cup dark molasses
¼ teaspoon salt
1 tablespoon rum
1 tablespoon grated orange rind
⅓ cup flaked coconut

Preheat oven to 375°.
Lay bananas in a shallow baking dish. Combine butter, molasses, salt, rum, and rind. Spoon over bananas. Sprinkle with coconut. Bake 15 minutes, basting 3 times while baking.
Serves 6 to 8.

This may be prepared in a chafing dish at the table. Simmer until bananas are tender.

Flaming Peaches

½ cup granulated sugar
¼ teaspoon cinnamon
½ lemon
8 well-drained peach halves
16 ice cream balls (or scoops)
½ cup red currant jelly
½ cup Burgundy
¼ cup warm brandy

On a dessert tray arrange a small dish containing the sugar and cinnamon, mixed together; the ½ lemon; a dish with the drained peaches; and a bowl with the ice cream balls. Prepare at the table. In a chafing dish over direct flame place the jelly and Burgundy. Dissolve the jelly, stirring. Add the sugar-cinnamon mixture and heat until steaming. Squeeze the juice of the ½ lemon into the chafing dish. Carefully spoon the peaches into the mixture, warming through. Heat the serving spoon over the flame, then pour a small amount of the brandy into the spoon. Ignite it and pour into the peaches and sauce, flaming. Immediately pour the rest of the brandy into the peaches. Stir and baste the peaches until flame subsides. Spoon ice cream into bowls and top with peach halves and sauce.
Serves 6 to 8.

Cold Orange Soufflé

3 egg yolks
½ cup sugar
grated rind of 3 oranges (about 2 tablespoons)
¾ cup fresh orange juice
1 tablespoon unflavored gelatin
¼ cup cold water
3 egg whites
2 cups heavy cream
1 can (11 ounces) drained mandarin orange slices

In a large bowl, beat the yolks and sugar with an electric beater for 5 minutes on medium speed. Stir in orange rind and orange juice. Soften gelatin in cold water and heat in a double boiler over hot water until thoroughly dissolved. Beat into egg mixture.

In a separate bowl whip egg whites until very stiff. In another bowl whip 1⅓ cups of the cream until stiff. Fold egg whites and whipped cream alternately into egg mixture. Transfer to a serving dish and chill until set.

At serving time whip remaining ⅔ cup cream and spread decoratively over top of soufflé. Arrange orange slices on top. Serves 6 to 8.

Pineapple-Lime Sherbet

1 cup boiling water
¾ cup sugar
1 package (3 ounces) lime Jell-O
juice and rind of 2 large lemons
1 can (8½ ounces) crushed pineapple
3 cups milk

Pour boiling water over sugar and Jell-O. Dissolve; add lemon juice and grated rind. Stir well. Add pineapple and milk. Freeze in a 2-quart container. After it is frozen solid, beat thoroughly or use a blender, then refreeze. The mixture must be thoroughly beaten after it first freezes.
Serves 12.

Lemon Velvet Ice Cream

5⅓ cups heavy cream
5⅓ cups milk
1¼ cups lemon juice
4 cups sugar
2 teaspoons lemon extract
1 tablespoon grated lemon rind

Mix all ingredients thoroughly. Pour into ice cream freezer and freeze according to manufacturer's directions.
Makes 3½ quarts.

If ice cream freezer cannot accommodate the mixture all at one time, half may be refrigerated for later freezing.

Coconut Ice Cream

1½ quarts light cream
2 cups milk
1½ cups sugar
⅛ teaspoon salt
5 eggs plus 5 egg yolks
2 tablespoons cornstarch
2 cups heavy cream
1 tablespoon vanilla
2 cups grated coconut

In a heavy 4-quart saucepan, heat the cream, milk, sugar, and salt, stirring until the sugar dissolves. In a separate bowl, beat the eggs, egg yolks, and cornstarch. Beat in a little of the hot cream, then add the egg mixture to the saucepan, stirring constantly. Cook over low heat for 10 minutes. Cool. Whip heavy cream and add with the vanilla to egg custard. Pour into an ice cream freezer and freeze according to manufacturer's instructions. Churn until mixture thickens. Add coconut and continue churning until firm.
Makes 1 gallon.

Mrs. Cliff Robertson (Dina Merrill) remembers that this was one of her mother's favorites.

Cheesecake Bars

5 tablespoons butter
⅓ cup brown sugar
1 cup sifted flour
¼ cup chopped walnuts
½ cup sugar
1 package (8 ounces) softened cream cheese
1 egg
2 tablespoons milk
1 tablespoon lemon juice
½ teaspoon vanilla

Preheat oven to 350°.
In mixing bowl, cream butter and brown sugar. Add flour and nuts. Mix well. Set aside 1 cup of this mixture for topping. Press

remainder in bottom of an 8 x 8 x 2 pan. Bake 12 to 15 minutes.

Blend sugar and cream cheese until smooth. Add egg, milk, lemon juice, and vanilla. Beat well. Spread over bottom crust. Sprinkle with the reserved cup of topping. Return to oven and bake 25 minutes longer. Allow to cool, then chill.

Yields 16 bars.

French Lace Cookies

1 cup unsifted flour
1 cup pecans, finely chopped
½ cup butter
½ cup light or dark corn syrup
⅔ cup brown sugar, packed

Preheat oven to 325°.

In a large mixing bowl, combine the flour and chopped nuts. Place the butter, syrup, and sugar in a saucepan. Bring to a boil, then remove from heat. Cool. Combine this with flour and nuts. Mix well. Drop by teaspoonfuls, 4 inches apart, on a well-greased cookie sheet (8 cookies to a sheet). Bake 8 to 10 minutes. Cookies will be very thin. Allow to cool 2 minutes before removing from pan.

Yields 3 dozen.

Pralines

3 cups sugar
1 cup buttermilk
1 teaspoon soda
8 tablespoons butter
dash of salt
2 tablespoons light or dark corn syrup
1 teaspoon vanilla
2 to 3 cups chopped pecans

In a deep saucepan over medium heat, mix sugar, buttermilk, soda, butter, salt, and corn syrup. Stir until it reaches a soft ball stage (234° on a candy thermometer). Remove from heat. Beat in

vanilla and pecans until mixture begins to thicken. Working quickly, drop by teaspoonfuls onto waxed paper and cool.
Yields 30 to 35.

Old-Fashioned Raisin Bars

1 cup seedless raisins
1 cup water
½ cup vegetable oil
1 cup sugar
1 egg, slightly beaten
1¾ cups sifted flour
1 teaspoon baking soda
¼ teaspoon salt
1 teaspoon cinnamon
½ teaspoon cloves
½ teaspoon nutmeg
½ teaspoon allspice
confectioner's sugar

Preheat oven to 375°.
In a saucepan, combine raisins and water. Bring to a boil. Remove from heat and stir in oil. Cool to lukewarm. Stir in sugar and egg. Sift together dry ingredients and beat into raisin mixture. Pour into a greased 13 x 9 x 2 pan and bake 20 minutes or until done. When cool cut into bars. Dust with confectioner's sugar.
Yields 24 bars.

Plantation Cake

1 cup butter
2 cups plus 4 teaspoons sugar
2 eggs
1 cup commercial sour cream
½ teaspoon vanilla
2 cups flour
1 teaspoon baking powder
¼ teaspoon salt
1 cup chopped pecans
1 teaspoon cinnamon

Preheat oven to 350°.

In a large mixing bowl, cream butter, adding 2 cups of the sugar gradually, beating until very light and fluffy. Beat in eggs, one at a time. Stir in the sour cream and vanilla. Fold in the flour, which has been sifted with the baking powder and salt. Combine the remaining sugar, pecans, and cinnamon. Place ⅓ of the batter in a well-greased 9-inch tube pan. Sprinkle with ¾ of the pecan mixture. Spoon in the remaining ⅔ batter. Sprinkle with remaining pecans and sugar and bake 60 minutes or until done. Cool on a rack.

Serves 10 to 12.

This cake is usually served with morning coffee or afternoon tea.

Fresh Apple Cake

3 cups flour
1 teaspoon baking soda
1 teaspoon salt
1¼ cups vegetable oil
2 cups sugar
3 eggs, well-beaten
3 cups thinly sliced, cored, and peeled apples
1 cup pecans, chopped
1 teaspoon vanilla

Caramel Topping

¾ cup butter
1½ cups light brown sugar
¼ cup plus 2 tablespoons evaporated milk
1 teaspoon vanilla

To prepare cake sift flour in a large mixing bowl. Measure and add the soda and salt. Sift again. Mix oil and sugar in a separate bowl. Add the eggs. Slowly stir in flour. Add apples, nuts, and vanilla and mix well. Pour into a greased 9 x 13 pan. Place in a cold oven, then turn to 325°. Bake 45 minutes or until it begins to shrink from sides of pan and springs back if pressed with finger.

To prepare topping melt the butter and sugar over low heat in medium saucepan. Add milk and bring to a full boil. Cook 1 minute, stirring. Add vanilla and cool to spreading consistency. Spread over cake and cut in the pan.

Yields 18 squares, 3 x 2 each.

Almond Cheesecake

Crust

1½ cups graham cracker crumbs
2 tablespoons sugar
1 teaspoon flour
¼ cup melted butter

Filling

2 pounds cream cheese, softened
1 cup sugar
2 eggs
½ teaspoon vanilla
½ teaspoon almond extract

Topping

1 pint sour cream
¾ cup sugar
¾ teaspoon almond extract
½ teaspoon lemon juice

Preheat oven to 350°.

Combine all ingredients for crust in a medium mixing bowl. Press into a 10-inch springform pan. Bake for 5 minutes. Remove from oven and allow to cool. Turn off oven and open door to cool.

Mix all ingredients for filling in a bowl and pour into the cooled crust. Place in cold oven and turn to 350°. Bake ½ hour.

Combine all topping ingredients and pour over baked cheesecake. Return to oven for 8 minutes longer. Chill overnight.

Serves 18 to 20.

Celestial Ice Cream Cake

1 10-inch angel food cake
2 pints coffee brandy ice cream, softened
1 cup coarsely chopped pecans
1 can (16 ounces) fudge topping
1 package fluffy white icing

Cut a 1-inch layer from top of angel food cake and reserve. Hollow out remaining cake to within 1 inch of bottom, leaving 1¾-inch rim around the outer and inner edges. Spread 1 pint of ice cream evenly into the hollowed shell. Sprinkle with pecans. Spread remaining ice cream smoothly on top of pecans. Replace top cake layer and place in freezer. Prepare icing according to package directions. Remove cake from freezer and frost top and sides. Decorate top with some of the fudge topping drizzled on from a spoon. Cover and store in freezer until 15 minutes before serving. Slice and serve with remaining fudge topping in a separate bowl.
Serves 10 to 12.

Mother Reynolds' Chocolate Cake

1 cup sifted cake flour
2 cups sugar
¼ teaspoon salt
½ cup dry cocoa
11 egg whites (1½ cups)
1 teaspoon cream of tartar
1 cup quartered maraschino cherries or finely chopped nuts

Preheat oven to 325°.
Sift together 5 times the flour, sugar, salt, and cocoa. Set aside.
In a large mixing bowl, beat the egg whites until foamy. Add the cream of tartar and continue beating at high speed until the whites are stiff but not dry. Carefully fold in the dry ingredients. Add vanilla and stir only until blended. Pour one quarter of the batter into an ungreased angel food cake pan. Sprinkle with one third of the cherries. Pour another quarter of the batter into the pan

and sprinkle with another third of the cherries. Repeat these steps, ending with the batter on top. Bake for 1 hour. Cool inverted. Serves 10 to 12.

This chocolate angel food cake was a special favorite at the Lenten teas in the thirties. It is also good covered with a chocolate icing.

Coconut Pound Cake

1 cup butter, softened
½ cup vegetable shortening
3 cups sugar
6 eggs
3 cups all-purpose flour
1 teaspoon vanilla
1 teaspoon lemon extract
1 tablespoon coconut flavoring
1 teaspoon almond extract
1 cup milk
1 can (3½ ounces) flaked coconut

Preheat oven to 325°.
In a large mixing bowl, cream the butter and shortening with the sugar. Add eggs one at a time, beating well after each addition. Add the flour and remaining liquid ingredients. Fold in the coconut and place mixture into a greased tube pan. Bake 1½ hours. Serves 10 to 12.

Jack's Favorite Cake

2 cups flour
1½ cups sugar
1 teaspoon baking soda
1 teaspoon salt
1 teaspoon cinnamon
1 teaspoon nutmeg
1 cup vegetable oil
½ cup buttermilk
3 eggs
1 cup stewed pitted prunes, chopped
1 cup chopped pecans
1 teaspoon vanilla

Sauce

1 cup sugar
½ cup butter
½ cup buttermilk
1 teaspoon baking soda

Preheat oven to 350°.

In a large mixing bowl, sift together the flour, sugar, soda, salt, cinnamon, and nutmeg. Add the oil, buttermilk, and eggs and mix well. Stir in the prunes, nuts, and vanilla. Pour mixture into a greased and floured 13 x 9 baking pan. Bake 35 to 40 minutes.

To prepare sauce combine all of the sauce ingredients in a saucepan and bring to a boil, stirring constantly. While cake is still hot, prick the top in several places with a fork. Pour the warm sauce over the warm cake. Cool and cut in the pan.

Makes 18 squares, 3 x 2.

This rich moist cake is a special nineteenth-hole treat of golfer Jack Nicklaus.

Island Rum Cake

1 cup butter
1½ cups sugar
4 eggs
2 cups flour
2 teaspoons rum flavoring
2 teaspoons baking powder
2 cups chopped pecans

Sauce
¾ cup sugar
½ cup water
½ cup light rum

Preheat oven to 325°.

In a large bowl, cream butter and sugar well with an electric mixer. Add eggs and mix until smooth. Add the flour and rum flavoring. Add the baking powder. Stir in the nuts. Grease and flour a tube pan. Pour mixture into pan and bake 1 hour on bottom rack of oven.

While cake is baking, prepare the sauce. In a medium saucepan, combine the sugar and water. Let it boil until sugar is dissolved. Remove from heat and add rum. While cake is still warm, pour on the warm rum sauce. After sauce is absorbed, invert on serving plate.

Serves 10 to 12.

Apple Tart

6 large apples (such as Golden Delicious) peeled, cored, and cut into ¼-inch slices
1 tablespoon sugar
1 9-inch unbaked pastry shell
¾ cup apricot preserves, pressed through a sieve

Preheat oven to 400°.

If apples are soft or particularly juicy, place slices in a bowl, sprinkle with sugar, and let stand 20 minutes. Prick bottom of pastry shell with a fork at ½-inch intervals. Line with buttered foil, fitted well into sides, and fill with dried beans. Bake 8 to 9 minutes until set but not brown. Remove beans and foil liner, prick again if necessary to prevent dough from rising, and bake 2 to 3 minutes longer. Cool.

Prepare glaze by melting in a small saucepan the sieved jam and the sugar or the juices drained from the sugared apples. Cook, stirring, until mixture coats the spoon lightly. Brush partially baked shell with warm glaze, covering bottom completely. Arrange drained apple slices in overlapping layers in spiral concentric circles. Return to oven for 15 to 20 minutes until apples are just tender and pastry browned. Remove from oven. Spoon or brush remaining warm glaze over apples. Serve tart hot or cool.

Key Lime Pie

3 eggs
1 cup sugar
⅓ cup key lime juice
2 tablespoons butter, melted
8-inch pie shell, unbaked

Preheat oven to 325°.

In a large bowl, beat eggs slightly. Add sugar, lime juice, and butter. Beat well. Pour into the pie shell. Bake 20 to 25 minutes until set. Top will be somewhat brown. Serve hot or cold.

Serves 6 to 8.

Menus

for Every Occasion

AFTER THE GAME
*Cold Madras Soup
*Carbonnade à la Flamande
*Spinach Mousse
*Almond Cheesecake

AFTER THE THEATER
*Mushroom Strudel
*Happy Warrior Scampi
*Asparagus and Avocado Salad
Hot Bread
*Flaming Peaches

AFTERNOON TEA
Tea Sandwiches
Fresh Fruit
*Mother Reynolds' Chocolate Cake
Toasted English Muffins with
    Marmalade
Tea and Coffee

BACK FROM THE BEACH
*Fairbanks Chowder
*Ziti à la Carbonara
*Ports of Call Salad
Hot Bread
Fresh Fruit in Season
*Pralines

BRIDGE LUNCHEON
*Zucchini with Sauce Tartare
*Seafood Quiche
*Masked Figs

BRUNCH
*Monterey Jack Eggs
*Plantation Cake
*Sun Ray Compote

BUFFET
*Mushroom Salad
*Ratatouille
Green Salad
Hot Rolls
*Strawberries on Ice

CAMPER PICNIC
*Crabmeat Soup (Cold or Hot)
*Moore-Betty Chicken (Cold or Hot)
*Salad Romano
Assorted Rolls
*Coconut Pound Cake

CHRISTMAS EVE DINNER
*Striped Avocado Soup
*Braised Pork with Caraway Seeds
Noodles
*Broccoli Amandine
*Cold Orange Soufflé

DERBY DAY DINNER
*Spinach Cheese Squares
*Kentucky Quail
Wild Rice
*Corn Pudding
*Island Rum Cake

DINNER ABOARD
*Cold Seafood with *Mustard Sauce
*Roast Beef Salad
Assorted Rolls
Fresh Pineapple Boats Flavored
with Kirsch

DINNER AT EIGHT
*Scampi Hollandaise
*Rack of Lamb
*Delmonico Potatoes
*Carrots John
Green Salad
Hot Bread
*Apple Tart

DINNER FOR A CROWD
*Parsnip Soup
*Osso Buco
Steamed Rice
*Italian Spinach Pie
Green Salad
*Cheesecake Bars

DIXIE DINNER
*Cream of Zucchini Soup
*Quail over the Coals
*Hominy Grits Soufflé
Green Salad
*Blueberries and Banana Cream

EASTER DINNER
*Watercress Soup (cold)
*Lamb Puccini
Green Salad
*Potatoes Italian
*Cold Chocolate Cream

*Recipe to be found in appropriate section.

FLORIDA SUMMER SUPPER
*Cream of Spinach Soup
*Summer Rice
*Broiled Mackerel with Mango
 Chutney
 Hot Bread
*Key Lime Pie

FORMAL DINNER
*Kimberly's Scalloped Oysters
*Truffled Tournedos
*Eggplant Soufflé
 Green Salad
*Bananas Tropicale

INTIMATE DINNER
*Queen Victoria Green Pea Soup
*Steak Diane
*Squash Gratiné
 Green Salad
 Hot Bread
*Chocolate Almond Soufflé

ITALIAN DINNER
*Baked Clams
*Scallopine à la Marsala
 Green Noodles
*Vegetables Vinaigrette
*Almond Cheesecake

NINETEENTH-HOLE DINNER
*Mushroom Soup Citron
*Roast Beef
*Oyster Casserole
*Fanned Zucchini
*Jack's Favorite Cake

OUTDOOR DINNER PARTY
 Crabmeat Soup (Cold or Hot)
*Flank Steak à la Mimbo
*Baked Rice, Tomatoes, and Cheese
*Watercress Salad
*Heavenlies

POOLSIDE DINNER
*Indian River Soup
*Dudley's Dove
*Persian Rice
*Avocado and Grapefruit Salad
*Lemon Velvet Ice Cream
*French Lace Cookies

POOLSIDE LUNCHEON
* Artichokes Stuffed with Shrimp
 Salad
 Assorted Rolls
*Fresh Apple Cake

SOUTH OF THE BORDER
*Gazpacho
*Lilly Pulitzer's Baked Chicken
*Black Beans José
 Green Salad
* Guava Shells with Creamed Cheese

STAG NIGHT
*Cream Olga
*Grilled Wild Duck
 Wild Rice
*Como's Cabbage
*Coconut Ice Cream

SUNDAY-NIGHT SUPPER
*Pozole
 Hard Rolls
*Pineapple-Lime Sherbet

TENNIS PARTY
 Cold Shrimp with *Sauce Scandia
*Lasagna with White Sauce
*Spinach Salad
 Hot Bread
*Celestial Ice Cream Cake

VIP DINNER
*Purée of Lima Bean Soup
*Chicken Alaska
*Tomatoes Florentine
 Green Salad
*Galliano Compote

Acknowledgments

Part One

MR. M. P. ANTHONY, former mayor of West Palm Beach and member of a pioneer family

MRS. ROSCOE TATE ANTHONY, member of a pioneer family

MRS. MAXINE BANASH, secretary of the Historical Society of Palm Beach Cour

MR. GRANT R. BEDFORD, executive director emeritus of the Henry Morrison Flagler Museum

MR. T. DENNIE BOARDMAN, a resident of Palm Beach for many years

MR. TOM BOHNE, Colonel Bradley's valet and right-hand man

MR. AND MRS. WALTER BROOKS. Mr. Brooks is the grandson of Mrs. Eva Stotesbury.

MRS. JOHN R. DUBOIS, member of a pioneer family in the Jupiter area. She has published a book on famous local shipwrecks.

MRS. D. F. DUNKLE, member of the Brelsford family who grew up in the historic Brelsford house

MR. CAMILE GABET, waiter at Bradley's from 1937 to 1942

MR. NICK GARA, manager of the Palm Beach Country Club and formerly connected with the Patio Restaurant

MRS. GLADYS GILLILAND, member of the cottage colony in the twenties

MRS. MIRIAM GRAHAM, friend of Addison Mizner's

MR. FRANK HENNESSY, Henry Flagler's office boy, who knew Mary Lily Flagler very well

MRS. ALFRED G. KAY, friend of Paris Singer

JUDGE JAMES R. KNOTT, president emeritus of the Historical Society of Palm Beach County, who checked the manuscript for accuracy

MR. RAY KUNKEL, former president of the Palm Beach Civic Association

MR. HOMER LARGE, ex-chief of the Palm Beach police department

MRS. GRACIA LEATH, member of the hotel society in the twenties and a member of the cottage colony in the late twenties and early thirties

MRS. NADINE LIVINGSTON, Mrs. Post's cook

MISS CATHRYN MCELROY, curator of the Henry Morrison Flagler Museum

MR. PAUL MADDOCK, member of a pioneer family

MRS. FLAGLER MATTHEWS, granddaughter of Henry Flagler

MR. FRANK MOFFAT, Mrs. Post's majordomo

MR. TOM T. REESE, JR., member of a pioneer family

MR. JOE RISDEN, owner of a Palm Beach restaurant famous in the twenties and thirties

MRS. CLIFF ROBERTSON, DINA MERRILL, daughter of Mrs. Marjorie Merriweather Post
MR. AND MRS. MORTIMER SACHS, who live in Addison Mizner's former penthouse
MR. CHARLES B. SIMMONS, executive director of the Henry Morrison Flagler Museum
MRS. H. ALPINE SMITH, friend of Mrs. Horace Dodge and Addison Mizner

Part Two

MRS. JAMES AKSTON
MRS. CHARLES AMORY
MRS. H. LOY ANDERSON
MR. NATHAN APPLEMAN
MRS. NORBERTO AZQUETA
MRS.. GEORGE W. BLABON
MR. AND MRS. WILLIAM E. BUCKLEY
MRS. PERRY COMO
MRS. ALVA CUDDEBACK
MRS. BEDFORD DAVIE
MR. MORTON DOWNEY
MRS. GUILFORD DUDLEY, JR.
MRS. NICHOLAS DU PONT
MRS. ELENA ECHARTE
MRS. DOUGLAS FAIRBANKS, JR.
MRS. ALFONSO FANJUL
MRS. ALFONSO FANJUL, JR.
MRS. JOSE PEPE FANJUL
MRS. ALBERTO FARINAS
MRS. ANDREW A. FRASER
MRS. LILLY FULLER
MRS. ROBERT GARDINER
GENERAL BRADLEY GAYLORD
MRS. F. WARRINGTON GILLET, JR.
MR. MARSHALL GRANT
MRS. WALTER S. GUBELMANN
MRS. ENID A. HAUPT
MRS. Augustine HEALY
DR. W. CARLOS HEATON
MR. DOUG HENDERSON
MR. AND MRS. PHILIP HULITAR
MR. WILLIAM E. HUTTON III

MRS. ELLIS JOHNSON
MRS. JOSEPH P. KENNEDY
MR. AND MRS. A. ATWATER KENT, JR.
MR. JAMES KIMBERLY
MRS. RUSSELL KUHNER
MR. AL McCLANE
MRS. M. H. McLEAN
MRS. FLAGLER MATTHEWS
MRS. DANIEL MORAN
MR. AND MRS. JACK NICKLAUS
THE HONORABLE BENJAMIN OEHLERT
MRS. JAMES O'SULLIVAN
MRS. IVA PATCEVITCH
MRS. M. WHARTON PETTIBONE
MRS. COSTANZO PUCILLO
MRS. SAMUEL RAUTBORD
MRS. WILEY REYNOLDS
MRS. PAUL ROGERS
MR. PHIL ROMANO
LADY ROTHERMERE
MRS. ENRIQUE ROUSSEAU
MR. JOHN RYBOVICH, JR.
MRS. STEPHEN SANFORD
MRS. GEORGE SCHRAFFT
MRS. THOMAS SHEVLIN
MRS. EARL E. T. SMITH
MRS. ROSA TUSA
MR. HECTOR UBERTALLI
MRS. ZOE SHIPPEN VARNUM
MR. HENRY WARREN
MRS. ROBERT WILMOTH
MRS. WILLIAM T. YOUNG, JR.

Photographs

Mrs. Elise Beale
Mr. and Mrs. Walter Brooks
Bob Davidoff Studios

The Henry Morrison Flagler Museum
Mr. Merrill Green
Historical Society of Palm Beach County
Mr. Bruce Hubbard

Mr. Joe Westly Jones
Mrs. Alfred G. Kay
Mort Kaye Studio
Mrs. Gracia Leath

Mr. Paul Maddock
Mr. Jack Maitland
Mr. Sam Quincey

The Junior League of the Palm Beaches, Inc., would like to thank its members and their friends who contributed so much to this book. Special thanks are due to Mrs. Thomas M. Mettler and Mrs. Marshall M. Criser, Jr., who served as presidents of the Junior League of the Palm Beaches, Inc., during the period when this book was written.

INDEX OF NAMES

INDEX OF RECIPES

236

239